e Full

Ulster

Fry

'Being an international superstar means I'm constantly on the move. My favourite way of keeping up with all events Norn Irish is The Ulster Fry. It's even better than the *Coleraine Chronicle*.'

JAMES NESBITT, OBE, INTERNATIONAL SUPERSTAR

'Events have conspired throughout history to give the people of Norn Iron a keenly wicked sense of humour, which has reached its dark zenith in the brilliant work by the team at The Ulster Fry.'

PHILL JUPITUS, COMIC LEGEND

'The Ulster Fry. So funny I might steal some of their brilliant jokes ... well, I say "might" ...'

TIM McGARRY, NATIONAL TREASURE

'Part of a balanced diet for anyone falling into the trap of taking NI politics too seriously!'

MICK FEALTY, POLITICAL GURU, SLUGGER O'TOOLE

'CSI Plumbridge, Pure Derry … and now The Ulster Fry. Maybe evolution does exist after all. We need satire. More than most places and The 'Fry has now earned its place as our foremost satirical staple.'

MARK PATTERSON, BBC BROADCASTER AND LOCAL HERO

The Full Ulster Fry

·THE·
BLACK
·STAFF·
PRESS

First published in 2018 by
Blackstaff Press
an imprint of Colourpoint Creative Ltd
Colourpoint House
Jubilee Business Park
21 Jubilee Road
Newtownards
BT23 4YH

Designed by seagulls.net
Printed in Northern Ireland by W&G Baird

ISBN 978-0-85640-993-6

www.blackstaffpress.com
www.theulsterfry.com

Contents

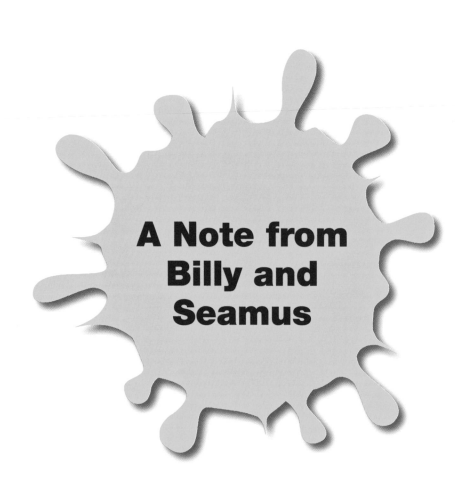

A Note from Billy and Seamus

The
Ulster
Fry

When we got together to start making up shite for the internet we never expected to have to write the introduction to one book, never mind two, but here we are … with all the best bits from the last couple of years.

For most of that time, Stormont has been suspended, but there's still been plenty happening – Brexit, RHI, elections, more elections. We got to make a load of silly fillums with top stars like Carl Frampton, Rory Best, Sir Jackie Fullerton and Pamela Ballantine. Seamus has even managed to have a baby somewhere along the way.

Inevitably with all that going on there's a whole load more people to thank:

The extended *Ulster Fry* team, including Paul, Andrew and Jemma; regular contributors like Keith, Colin and Cathaoir; plus anyone who has sent us their ideas.

At Smarts Communicate, thanks to Cahir, Jill, Claire, Emma and Lauren, who keep reminding us to do stuff. Jeanette and Lauren at Harp who make our fillums possible. We've worked with half the young acting talent of NI, but special thanks to Johnny, Oisin, Brendan and Katie, who've all agreed to risk career suicide by regularly taking part in our shite.

Huge thanks also to our friends and families for providing us with so much support over the years. All the time you spent listening to us moan when no one read something we'd spent ages on didn't (ironically) go unnoticed.

Also a special mention for Patsy and the team at Blackstaff Press who, for some reason, agreed to work with us again, despite us being the most disorganised writers in the entire world.

Genuine thanks to all our readers as well. Somehow you've managed to keep us going despite the evil machinations of Mark Zuckerberg.

But most of all we have to say a heartfelt thank you to Arlene and Michelle, and Ian and Gerry, for all the inspiration.

The
Ulster
Fry

Sausages

The 8 REAL reasons why Norn Iron is the happiest place in the UK

Northern Ireland
It's not as bad as you'd think

discover norniron .com

People across the Province let out a collective 'ye wha?' today after Northern Ireland was declared the 'happiest place in the UK' by a well-being survey.

'Ye sure it wasn't a survey of unwell-beings?' joked Tyrone resident Carol Gas. 'Sure ye canny even get a decent phone signal in this neck of the woods, and all we do is argue about whether we're in the UK in the first place,' she told us, by postcard.

Despite this complaint, we've had a look at some of the main reasons Norn Iron people are so happy.

Our excellent transport network............

Covering an astounding three counties of our sprawling Province, NI Railways allow passengers to visit places cars have been avoiding for generations. Our road system is no less impressive, featuring innovative bits of tarmac for tractors to pull into so you can overtake. Shame no one ever uses them.

The marching season..

Tourists flock to Northern Ireland every year to celebrate the Twelfth of July, which begins in February and ends roughly around September. It's one day you don't want to miss!

Our healthy diet ....

Foreign types used to the unhealthy Mediterranean diet must be so jealous of our life-enhancing foods. From brown lemonade to Spicy Bikers, our traditional dishes are packed full of all the preservatives and additives necessary to ensure a balanced diet.

Larne ....

The survey claims that Larne people are the happiest in the country. This also makes everyone else happy because if Larne wasn't there, its people might end up living near the rest of us.

The lovely weather ....

Northern Ireland gets more *Sun* than any other region in the UK. We also get the *Daily Mirror*, the *Guardian*, and the *Belfast Telegraph*. Usually cos it's too wet to go outside and they have football in them.

Great job opportunities ....

With the abundance of jobs in call centres with zero-hour contracts, NI folk love the monthly heart-attack feeling of wondering if they should pay their mortgages or feed their kids. Where else in the world can you phone your own call centre to see where your tax credits are, then turn yourself down?

Lack of English people ....

One of the great things about not living in England is not living with English people. Recent census data has revealed that Northern Ireland is primarily populated by people from Northern Ireland, who according to a survey taken amongst ourselves, range from being 'dead on' and 'quare craic' to 'wile sound'.

Our system of government ....

The rest of the planet looks on in envy at the workings of Stormont, one of the great beacons of world democracy. The standard of debate is unmatched – if the House of Commons is the Mother of all Parliaments, then Stormont has to be the Muthaf**ka.

Man who invented predictive text pisses away quietly in his sleep

The world of information technology was plunged into mourning today after the untimely death of one of its greatest figures.

According to his family, Brian Sturgeon – also known as Brain Surgeon – died at 6 a.m. this morning 'after a shirt I'll nest' and will be 'sourly mist'.

Giants of the technology industry were quick to issue messages of condolence to the family. Bill Gates, the founder of Microsoft, tweeted, 'Brain was once of the Finnish mines of his germination, sum one

how made tack knoll or key more axe cess able to the horde in any man in the sheep.'

Similarly Mark Zuckerberg of Facebook was effusive in his praise.

'Without Brain their wood be no Fact boot,' he told his legion of followers. 'He made complete ideals simple, and allowances us all to commune

at gates more quickly in and even changing would.'

The passing of Mr Sturgeon, who friends say had just celebrated his 'farty sex birthday', follows closely on the heels of the tragic death of Yokahama Mitsubishi, the inventor of the emoticon, who died in a car crash in Tokyo yesterday morning.

Hundreds of sad face smileys have poured in from across the world, and the Japanese government has announced a three-day period of national thumbs down emoji.

Bangor replaces Hillsborough as 'Town most up its own hole' at annual awards

The North Down town of Bangor has beaten its traditional rival Hillsborough to the coveted title of 'Town most up its own hole, 2018' at the annual 'Holey' awards.

Hillsborough controversially scooped the prize last year, relegating Holywood and Crawfordsburn to silver and bronze. This year, however, the judges have praised 'the concerted effort of Bangor to get further up its own hole'.

'It's been a remarkable turnaround,' says the chair of the judging committee, Grant Causeway. 'The town has shown amazing resilience to come from nowhere to first place.'

The judges were particularly impressed by the way Bangor

thinks it's great, even though it's a bit shit. 'It has two train stations, a couple of marinas and stuff – even the shopping centres have posh names like Bloomfield and Flagship. But the Flagship Centre is actually worse than Connswater, and that's some achievement.'

Independently Independent Unionist Lady Camilla Pickie-Park, who represents the affluent Bangor West ward on Ards and North Down Council, told us she was delighted at the news. 'We'd built up a reputation as a "go-to" destination in the summer months, so the council has

been working hard to make sure there's nothing to do when you get here.

'Hopefully this lack of investment can continue – we can't have the hoi polloi from the likes of Holywood and Newtownards cluttering up our shops, can we?'

Local resident Billy Holme-Beach was also pleased. 'I have a yacht,' he told us. 'A yacht.'

Representatives of the defeated Hillsborough team are understood to be furious, but vowed to bounce back. 'The Queen lives here for two days a year,' their campaign chief Hector Hamilton-Hunniford-Hill argued. 'How can those seaside plebs possibly out-hole us?

'We'll be pulling out all the stops next year, probably by announcing a Lobster and Champagne Festival in June.'

Hillsborough skeleton 'the poshest we've found' say archaeologists

The thousand-year-old skeleton unearthed in the grounds of Hillsborough Castle was wearing corduroy trousers and was buried in a Barbour-lined coffin, *The Ulster Fry* has learned.

According to the archaeologist in charge of the dig, people in ancient times were often buried with items that were significant to their lives. 'We can learn so much from these grave goods,' says Professor Walter Dolmen, 'and "Hillsborough Man" was surrounded by some very exciting finds.

'Look at the craftsmanship on this ancient polo mallet, and the design of these keys shows that he must have owned some kind of primitive Range Rover. We can only imagine the kinds of journeys he made in such a vehicle, probably leaving the boys to school at Inst and taking little Hermione to her horseriding lessons.'

These finds contrast with those found at similar sites across Northern Ireland. 'If we're excavating in Tyrone, for example, we'd expect to find the remains of baler twine tied round the waist of the skeleton,' explains the archaeologist. 'We might also find that the skull had an enlarged jaw, evidence that people couldn't understand a word he said – resulting in attempts to talk louder.'

Inevitably burial grounds in the Lurgan area contain primitive wine bottles, whilst Bronze Age chieftains in County Antrim are often found interred with several sheep, 'in case there were none in the next world'. West Belfast graves are rarely excavated due to the ancient custom of burying local men with an explosives cache.

Graves in Derry are the only exception. 'Generally we find nothing in the North-West,' says Professor Dolmen. 'Probably because, even then, themuns in Belfast got everything.'

Fears in Belfast that A6 road project may bring 'culchie invasion'

There is growing concern among Belfast residents that plans to improve the road link to the West may lead to some kind of culchie apocalypse.

For decades Belfast has managed to shield itself from the worst excesses of culchyism, mainly by ensuring that the road and rail links to Derry are as bad as possible. However the proposal to dual the road from Randalstown to Magherafelt will leave the city wide open to invasion.

'This is terrible news,' said Glengormley native Newton Abbey. 'They'll be down here in their thousands from places like Claudy and Donemana, wandering around in their checked shirts and stonewashed jeans, or cluttering up the roads with ancient tractors and Land Rovers.'

'The Derry ones will be worse,' claimed West Belfast woman Donna Falls. 'They'll be all, "What about ye, mucker, do you have any buns? Where canna git the *Journal*, hi?" I can't be arsed listening to them with their auld accents, so I can't.'

Belfast City Council is already planning defences against the expected hordes. 'We'll have checkpoints at Sandyknowes to test them for silage,' said Andy Knowles, the council's Head of Emergency Planning. 'Then inner defences at Duncrue Street consisting of a 50-foot-high steel wall with big flashing lights on top. I don't think they have electricity up there so hopefully they'll be frightened off.'

We spoke to some people West of the Bann using an elaborate system of cups on string, and they told us they had no plans to invade Belfast 'for the foreseeable future'.

'Why the f**k would ye want to go all the way up there, hi?' asked professional Derryman Séan Tallow. 'As anyone who has ever taken the train will tell ye … it's at least five hundred miles away!

'Plus, when ye do get there, they look at ye funny for ordering a sausage roll inside a bap. F**king weirdos.'

Northern Ireland's 10 most annoying road users

So Belfast is in the top ten most congested cities in the UK, making it one of the worst in Europe, and it's no wonder. Here's a rake of people who should be barred from the roads, according to my da anyway.

Taxis

The only motorists who don't seem to do a driving test. U-turns in the middle of the road and randomly dropping off fares on corners, combined with 2 a.m. horn blasting and a tendency to arrive an hour later than you booked give them a special place in all our hearts.

Pedestrians

Wandering aimlessly in front of traffic staring at their mobiles, then stopping to talk to their mates in the middle of a zebra crossing.

Lorries

Huge, lurching hoors that pull out in front of you and take three days to accelerate to 34 mph, but that can then reach breakneck speeds on the only straight bit of road where you could overtake. Load-shedding hallions of the highways.

Buses

Own the road, literally, with their private lanes and ability to block roads for twenty minutes while every idiot boarding attempts to pay with a £50 note. Would it be that hard to bring in 'exact change only' like normal countries?

Tractors ....

There are two types of tractors – massive bastard tractors with machinery too wide for the road that bate along at forty attempting to clean every other road user, and tiny Massey Fergusons driven at 3 mph by old men in flat caps who are out for a pint of milk but brought a dog and a bucket in the link box.

Boy Racers..

Souped-up, suspension-lowered, shite-music-blasting dicks, parked up talking crap after hoking down the back of the sofa to find £3 to buy petrol for their bright orange Vauxhall Novas. Eff all to do except rev their engines before doing donuts on the Glenshane, and forcing every estate in the country to have speed bumps.

Cyclists.....................................

Lycra-clad, arse-wobbling, pavement-mounting, non-indicating, two-abreast, lightless, self-righteous enviro-clampits.

Pensioners ....

Doing ten in a forty zone in a tiny Nissan Micra, half of them can hardly see over the steering wheel. If they're not causing traffic jams, they're riding on buses for free, expecting paying customers to give up their seats just because they were born shortly after a war. They never mention that they started the Troubles as well.

Women.....................................

Doing their make-up in the rear-view mirror while forgetting that lights change. Finding six empty parking spaces too tight to reverse into. Driving cars with names and getting cheaper insurance.

Men ....

Believe that they were born with in-built driving skills that make them superior to every other road user, but that leave them unable to either control rage or remember to indicate, particularly when driving a BMW.

That should cover everyone. You can be sure that the roads would be much quieter if all these ganches were banned from them.

Belfast to finally get 'Straight Pride' parade

After more than twenty years of complaining that there's no Straight Pride event to mirror Gay Pride, Belfast's homophobic community have finally got grant funding to hold their own parade.

As our poorly photoshopped image shows, the event will celebrate the very best of stereotypical straight male pursuits. The eager crowd will be able to enjoy an exciting parade with floats carrying things like garden sheds, angry dads drinking beer, air-guitar displays and fishing.

According to retired Free Presbyterian minister the Rev. David McIlspleen, religious fundamentalists will have their own special role. 'We're working on a float showcasing our finest street preachers, who'll rant loudly then sing badly using utterly inadequate sound systems, whilst colleagues hand out tracts for people to drop in the street.'

Unsurprisingly the gay community is up in arms about the news.

'I'm not heterophobic and some of my best friends are straight, but this is a step too far,' said gay rights worker Sebastian Muller. 'There's more than enough heterosexuality in the media, and to be frank, we're fed up with having this kind of stuff rammed down our throats 365 days a year.

'We'll be out in force at the City Hall gates to protest,' he continued. 'Mainly by looking fabulous.'

Third bus stop at Belfast International Airport approved

Northern Ireland's transport links moved proudly into the 1960s today with the approval of plans for a third bus stop at the world famous Belfast International Airport.

Tourists from across the globe regularly jet into the International Airport from far-flung destinations such as Manchester and Glasgow, but often spend their stay staring at the County Antrim countryside, believing that they are actually in Belfast itself.

However all this will now change, according to the airport's Head of Customer Disservice, Ellie Copter. 'The new stop will make the airport a transport hub for the Province, allowing weary travellers access to the best

attractions we have to offer,' she told us.

'Basically, you'll be able to simply step off a plane, wait in that cattle barn for your luggage for a bit then choose from three different places to go – most likely Belfast, Derry and Craigavon.'

The proposal is part of a multi-pound expansion plan for the airport, which experts feel will finally make it live up to the expectations of a twentieth-century traveller.

'There'll be at least three more bins, an extra cash point, and a new phone box,' Ms Copter revealed. 'We're also thinking of installing a cattle grid on the runway.'

Not to be outdone, their rivals at George Best City Airport have announced the installation of an extra toilet in their departure area, which they say will be specially reinforced to withstand dense and heavy waste.

When quizzed on the peculiar nature of this particular upgrade, Airport Manager Roe Heath told us, 'It's simple really. Most people shit a brick when they see the price of our food.'

Russian warships now refuelling at Muff Filling Station

Following today's intervention by NATO to block Russian warships from refuelling in Spain, *The Ulster Fry* has learned that the fleet was then diverted to the Derry/Donegal border to fill up at the world-famous Top Muff Filling Station.

'Vladimir Putin is a cunning and ruthless operator,' said CIA analyst Zach Crakensachs. 'Our intel suggests he ordered his fleet captains to "fill 'em to the throat" with a locka green diesel, instead of their preferred red variety. And then to make sure they got the change in euros – not sterling.

'Cos it's not worth pish,' he explained.

Whilst Spanish authorities steered clear of the controversy, Muff's Lord Mayor Pat McGarden said the town was 'delighted' with the influx of trade and that their guests had been 'very well behaved'.

'Not only did our Gerard pump over 475,000 litres of diesel today, but we sold about eight thousand pokes and God knows how many jambons and sausage rolls. Them boys can quare eat, hi.

'Not sure Mickey in the car wash is too happy, though,' he added. 'He had to power-wash three battleships for €12.50.'

The US government are understood to be monitoring the situation closely and has set up a joint task force with local fuel dipping agency VOSA to stop the Russian war effort in its tracks.

'Satellite reconnaissance indicates that they'll have to sail further into the North to

get turned, and when they do, BOOM – we're gonny dip the hoors,' said Dick Ballbag from VOSA. 'We'll just impound their ships there and then – unless they can pay £500 on the spot.'

'Mister Putin, me thinks we haz prøblem' admitted ship captain Dimitri Ballacheov, in a transmission we later intercepted. 'We haz spent all spare mønies øn free-statez Taytø and big fack-øff bøttles of Smirnøff wødka, sir.'

The owner of Muff Liquor refused to comment.

Anti-Trump rioting spreads to Ulster American Folk Park

With riots sweeping the US following the election of Donald Trump, protests have now reached our shores, with the PSNI reporting 'historically accurate civil unrest' at the Ulster American Folk Park.

'The election of Trump is an affront to the memory of Ulster emigrants who made the long journey to new, far-off lands,' said park re-enactor Penny Farthing.

'He's not our president, Lincoln is,' claimed the part-time yarn spinner, 'So we're not allowing any tourists in until he resigns. They just can f**k off back to where they came from.'

The PSNI have confirmed that rioting began in the park's 'Old World' area, before spreading across the Atlantic.

'It's pretty hostile in there,' confirmed Sergeant Barton Round from the PSNI's Historical Enquiries Team. 'We've seen a number of horses hijacked and several covered wagons have been set on fire. We haven't seen trouble like this since Ulysses S. Grant was elected President in 1869.'

Observers have reported seeing masked men firing

muskets from within the ranks of protesters, resulting in a cavalry charge from the PSNI mounted response unit. However the situation soon calmed when officers arrived with a cannon.

'The real McCoy,' says Sergeant Round. 'Not one of those wishy-washy water cannon yokes you see in Belfast.'

This is the worst case of historically-themed civil disorder in Northern Ireland since the famous Folk and Transport Museum riots of 1985, when six people were killed during protests against the Corn Laws.

Top 10 places to get clean soaked in Northern Ireland

There have been a lot of handy guides for tourists on social media recently, telling them the Top 10 eateries, bars or attractions in Northern Ireland, but here at *The Ulster Fry* we think they've been missing out on a key element of any visit to our shores – getting completely drenched in pissing rain.

So here it is – *The Ulster Fry* Top 10 list of places to get clean soaked …

1. Great Victoria Street...

Officially opened by Queen Victoria in 1923, Great Victoria Street is often the first stop-off point for tourists arriving in Belfast. As they emerge bleary-eyed off the 4.20 Goldliner from New York, eager to sip their first pint of Guinness in the Crown Bar, they are usually greeted by driving rain, coming horizontally along the street's famous wind tunnel. Other attractions include a wide variety of grey-faced

smokers lurking outside Caffè Nero, and at least five bus tour operatives waiting patiently to club them over the head and usher them on to number two on our list …

2. An open-top Bus Tour of Belfast ....

Who, in their wisdom, decided that it was a good idea to introduce the open-topped bus to our city streets? It's like constructing a soft-topped space shuttle, just in case the sun comes out on your journey through space. A guaranteed good Ulster soakin' for the unsuspecting tourist, at least until they hop off at our next destination …

3. Any Translink Bus Shelter...

The words 'bus' and 'shelter' should never be used together in Northern Ireland because these so-called shelters are, in fact, one- or two-sided structures carefully designed to leave the waiting commuter facing into the prevailing wind and inevitable rain. Good advice for any visitor is to stand behind the largest person you can find, who will probably be called Sammy or Sean, depending on which part of the city the bus is heading to.

4. Ravenhill Rugby Ground................................

It is often said that rugby is a game played by men with odd-shaped balls. This is because it is always bollock freezing and at the newly opened Kingspan Stadium you can be sure that the rain will be blowing straight into your face throughout the match. Best to stay under the stand in a bar.

5. The Giant's Causeway ....

Leaving Belfast, the Antrim coast is always popular with tourists, and NI's only World Heritage Site is usually top of the list. It shouldn't be, unless it is one of the two days of the year when the sun shines. Creationists believe the causeway was formed during the Great Flood, something that is easy to believe as you negotiate several thousand slippery blocks of basalt on a wet February excursion.

6. Dunluce Castle ....

Built by Ronald McDonald in 1534, Dunluce Castle is now best described as an 'impressive ruin'. This is because the incessant rain at the site has washed away most of the structure. Still nice to look at, mind you, from inside a car.

7. Derry's Walls..

Heading further along the coast, the intrepid visitor will eventually reach the Maiden City, where they will no doubt be enticed on to a tour of the famous city walls. They will soon learn that they are utterly devoid of shelter, and the mile-long circuit will feel much longer. The Bogside is so named for good reason – it was originally made up of marshy ground caused by the rivers of rainwater running down Butcher Street.

8. County Fermanagh..

Most of County Fermanagh is under water, and it is easy to see why. As soon as you cross into the county you will be met by vertical rain that will only stop when you leave. It is still well worth a visit, though: you can explore the Marble Arch Caves, in a boat.

9. The Mourne Mountains ....

Heading back east, any tourist eager for a bit of hillwalking should take in the Mourne Mountains. You should also bring several coats, so that you can replace each rain-sodden garment as it reaches saturation level.

10. Any Outdoor Event ....

Most outdoor events in Northern Ireland are held in the months of May and June. This is to try and catch the brief window of good weather that non-Irish people refer to as 'summer', and to avoid the traditional rioting season that kicks off in July. This usually fails, so your highly anticipated visit to the Tennent's Vital music festival will end up with you covering your pint during a deluge as you squint at a distant band performing on a rain-soaked stage.

 Or stay dry ...

So that's your list – but remember, it's not all bad. When it does rain, you can just go to the pub, preferably wearing one of our highly desirable T-shirts ...

Celebrations on Sesame Street as Gay Cake finally delivered

It was party time on New York's famous Sesame Street this morning after the cast of the hit show finally took delivery of Bert and Ernie's cake.

The so-called 'Gay Cake' was finally released from storage this morning after a prolonged legal wrangle, arriving on set just after 11 a.m.

'About f**king time,' said a disgruntled Ernie as he drank champagne from one of Big Bird's shoes. 'I ordered this for Bert's fortieth and he's forty-two now. We're gonna make up for lost time – eat the cake, get blocked and go clubbing.'

The joy was short-lived, however, as Elmo quickly pointed that the cake was

well past its sell-by date and virtually inedible.

'Not even Cookie Monster could eat that shite,' the red-furred Muppet told us, despite the fact his large blue colleague was shovelling the stale cake into his mouth as we spoke.

'Course I'll f**king eat it,' said Cookie Monster. 'It's a matter of principle and I won't let them bakers win this one.'

God, meanwhile, has moved (in a mysterious way) to assure his followers that there is no need to panic as a result of the court ruling.

'This does not mean you have to turn gay if you're not already gay,' he told us from a cloud. 'It is not a sign of the end of days and the four horsemen are still in the stables.

'Everyone should now just catch themselves on and try to show each other a wee bit of respect instead of just demanding it,' he continued.

'Or, to put it another way, stop trying to have your cake while eating it.'

Oscar the Grouch refused to comment.

Belfast descends into anarchy after bin day change

The United Nations has been forced to declare a state of emergency in Belfast after a change in the city's bin collection rota led to widespread disorder.

Attempts by the city council to roll out the new schedule ended in failure, with some disaster experts warning that up to 30 per cent of households didn't know what bin day it was.

'It's a crisis on a biblical scale,' said UN relief worker Cody Hannan. 'I've never seen suffering like it.'

Visibly traumatised, the exhausted UNICEF worker told us about some of the scenes he'd witnessed.

'There are families out there who don't know if it's recycling day,' he sobbed. 'I spoke to one pensioner whose brown bin hadn't been emptied in a week.'

A whole week – imagine that! When you opened the lid and stuck your head in you could smell it.'

Large parts of Belfast are now in a state of open revolt, and the authorities have admitted that they've lost control of the situation.

'It's anarchy out there,' says fellow UN worker Frankie Moon. 'Traffic is at a standstill;

hospitals are at breaking point; and armed gangs control many areas.'

However a spokesman for the Council assured us that this was all perfectly normal for Belfast, and urged everyone to 'calm their jets'.

'It's a change in the bin schedule,' he told us. 'We're not in f**king Aleppo.'

PSNI hire Batman to 'sort this clown sh*te out'

The PSNI has made a swift move to clamp down on so-called 'killer clowns' by hiring well-known superhero Batman to deal with the dicks behind it.

The craze, which began in America of course, involves arseholes dressing up as scary clowns then lurking in the shadows in an attempt to terrify passers-by.

'We didn't feel fully equipped to deal with this phenomenon,' says Superintendent James Gordon. 'We sought outside help and Mr Batman was the obvious choice, given his long history of dealing with scary-looking clown types like the Joker. Luckily for us he was at a loose end and agreed to come over.'

Batman had to undergo rigorous training to adapt to the PSNI's working practices.

'I spent three weeks at your training college,' he revealed, 'learning how to sit around on my hole drinking coffee while engaging in Facebook banter with other stations, as well as mastering the art of eating a Chinese takeaway in the back of a Land Rover. It went well, and I managed to put on three stone to reach the required weight for serving PSNI officers.'

The Dark Knight has now been unleashed on to the streets of Belfast to combat the craze, and intends to sort the problem in his own unique way.

'I'll just knock their ballix in,' he says. 'Folk here have had forty years of masked clowns terrorising them – they don't need any more of this shit.'

Superintendent Gordon has confirmed that if Batman is a success, the PSNI would consider hiring other fictional superheroes to deal with crime.

'We're in talks with Spiderman,' he told us. 'Apparently he has this thing called "Spidey sense" which might come in handy for dealing with wee hoods nicking cars.'

Local woman 'might not get redd up for Christmas'

There are growing concerns in religious circles that Antrim housewife Pauline Slooter may be unable to effectively tidy her house before Christmas, leading to fears that the festival may have to be cancelled altogether.

The Ulster Fry understands that Mrs Slooter inadvertently failed to fully 'redd out her good room' before putting up her decorations, leaving what has been described as a 'quare rake of clabber' behind the furniture. Now that the decorations are in place, it is virtually impossible for her to access the mounting filth.

'God knows what's behind the sofa,' she told us. 'It can't be moved for fear of wrecking the tree. I've had a good hoke down the back with the hoover but there's a fair amount of brock still in there. I'll never get it sorted before the in-laws come next Sunday.'

Mrs Slooter's situation mirrors a notorious incident from 2008 when Ballymoney woman, Fidelma Cracker, declared herself 'all set for Christmas' a full ten days in advance of the big day.

A subsequent investigation discovered that her announcement of her 'all-set' status was wildly premature – she'd forgotten to buy wrapping paper and hadn't ordered the turkey – forcing church leaders to consider moving Christmas to mid-January.

Fortunately, the crisis was averted when Mrs Cracker remembered that she'd stocked up on wrapping paper in the January sales and was actually going to her sister's for dinner.

12 unintentionally rude things we've seen on our travels

We're a pair of big weans here at *Ulster Fry* Towers, and like nothing better than a good snigger at something that might be a wee bit rude.

Because of this, we like to keep our cameras handy in case we spot anything sniggerable when we're on our travels, and since we've nothing else to put on these pages we thought we'd share them with you.

1. This old comic book ....
Billy bought this in a second-hand shop and was very disappointed by the contents.

2. This gatepost...............................
Okay, this one might be intentional, but every time we go to the Mournes it's a sniggerfest round the countryside with all these diddy gateposts.

3. This horseriding manual ....
Really? There was no other name they could have come up with?

4. These bath bombs
Not a very enticing offer.

5. This German ski-jumper ....
Must have been quare craic at school for this lad.

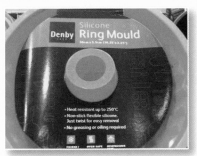

6. This thing in the Denby shop ....
Apparently if you go to the doctor you can get a cream to clear it up.

7. This pub door in Banbridge ....
What was on the designer's mind when he or she came up with this?

8. This special offer, also in Banbridge...................
Long queue outside this shop. The cheaper ones have more hair.

9. This unusual piece of exercise equipment.......
Being sold second-hand at Bangor Auctions. Not sure why anyone would want a second-hand hoop massager.

10. The judge at this cattle show ....
He seems to have got a bit close to the competitors.

A sweet young calf with tremendous ring presence was how judge ████████ described the Jersey champion at the 11th annual multi-breed calf show, held at Moira.
   Overall winner was the

11. The instructions on this Weetabix box ....
There's bound to be a better way of wording this.

12. And finally – the entire plumbing section of B&Q................
Is plumbing the most innuendo-laden trade out there?

Ards man who 'lost the run of himself' seeks help finding it

A forty-three-year-old Newtownards man who 'lost the run of himself' in the 1990s has appealed for more help for people suffering from the condition.

The man, who asked to be named, broke down as he told *The Ulster Fry* how the consequences of his mistake had gradually taken over his life.

'It began after I left university,' he revealed. 'I got a decent job, had a bit of money in the bank and all the trappings of wealth – the Ford Escort – Ghia of course – the posh apartment in Dundonald, even a caravan in Portrush. Before I knew it, people were saying "He's lost the run of himself." And you know what? I had.'

Since then, the man has struggled to cope with the debilitating symptoms of his illness, gradually upgrading to fancier four-wheel drive vehicles and even holidaying abroad, but now he's seeking help.

Dr Bud Pressure from the Ulster Hospital's Local Clichés Department says admitting you've a problem is the first step to recovery.

'Many people are completely unaware that they've lost the run of themselves,' he told us. 'They wear shoes with no socks, call their kids things like Hermione and go out for dinner more than once a month. These are clear warning signs.

'If they come to us, they can be treated,' he continued, 'mainly through "Catch Yourself On" therapy and a regular kick up the arse.'

Despite this, Dr Pressure agrees more needs to be done. 'The Executive needs to invest in awareness programmes,' he concluded. 'Though to be fair half of Stormont seems to suffer from the same condition.'

If you or any of your family have been affected by this story, help is out there. Call the 'Wind Yer Neck In, Big Lad' helpline on 0800 800 800 800 800 4.

Little Drummer Boy rerouted by Parades Commission

With less than six weeks till Christmas *The Ulster Fry* has learned that The Little Drummer Boy has already been controversially re-routed by the Parades Commission.

We understand that the boy had applied to the body to parade along his traditional route from North Belfast into the city centre, but has now been banned from passing the Ardoyne shops. Further restrictions are also in place, with the twelve-year-old told that he must only play a single drumbeat while passing St Patrick's Church on Donegall Street.

The boy's supporters have reacted angrily to the news, with former Demochristmas Unionist MLA Santa McClausland describing it as 'an appalling attack on our seasonal religious liberty'.

'I fully expect all right-thinking people to come on to the streets against this decision,' Mr McClausland told us. 'We will be establishing a Protest Grotto at Twaddell Avenue, and hanging Christmas decorations from all available lamp posts.'

This is not the first time that the commission has found itself embroiled in such musical controversy.

In 2008 the body prevented Elton John from making his traditional 'Step into Christmas', ordering him to walk through a different season altogether. Then in 2010 it banned Chris Rea from following his usual route on his drive home, resulting in the Teeside singer becoming hopelessly lost and ending up on 'The Road to Hell'.

'I just wanted to get home for Christmas,' he told us, 'I never expected to end up in Strabane.'

Belfast airport chaos as tray table isn't returned to upright position

Belfast International Airport was thrown into turmoil today when an aircraft broke down after a passenger decided to leave a plastic tray table dangerously hanging over their legs during landing.

The incident began at 6 a.m. this morning when panicked cabin crew realised that one passenger hadn't stowed their tray table away as instructed.

'I was already strapped in when I realised!' revealed flight attendant Celia Bordan-Paz. 'I was pure shiteing my bags, but thankfully the auld training kicked in and I was able to calm down and tell everyone to brace for impact.'

Unable to cope with the sheer aerodynamic down forces at work the plane naturally broke down upon landing. However a Civil Aviation Authority investigation into its black-box data has since revealed several other problems which contributed to NI's worst aviation incident in years.

'Thon boy in seat 12F had the blind down on his window,' says CAA spokesperson, Anita Bokebag. 'The fella next to him had his seat reclined a bit … and, according to the flight log, it seems at least three people were playing Candy Crush Saga despite being told to switch all devices off.'

A flight attendant revealed further passenger recklessness. 'Everyone was reading the in-flight magazine when I was explaining how to die properly at sea,' moaned Olga Hed-Lokker.

The airport was forced to close for several hours due to the incident, but normal service has now resumed and cabin crew are now back to doing what they do best.

'I'll mostly be standing in the doorway telling passengers which direction their seats are in, even though they can only go one way,' explained Hed-Lokker. 'But I'll also read out their seat number to them, just in case they can't read.'

The plane itself remains grounded amid reports that its badly damaged wheels are currently in the airport bar getting rubbered.

One wheel later released a statement saying, 'Yeeeeeoooo.'

Security alert online shuts Portrush Ghost Train

There is a security alert on the line at Barry's Amusements in Portrush, police have confirmed.

Officers say the track leading into the haunted house may be closed for some time while they ascertain whether it is a viable device.

A spokesman for the PSNI explained: 'We thank the public for their patience at this time, as this is a delicate operation and further complicated by the fact we're having wile bother finding a bomb disposal expert who isn't afraid of the dark.

'To be fair, it's bloody scary in there,' he added 'There's feckin cobwebs and everything.'

A spokesman for the bomb disposal unit said: 'Trying to remember whether to cut the blue wire or the green wire is a whole handlin' at the best of times, but it's even more of a pain in the hole when you are trying to cope with luminous cardboard cutouts whizzing past you going "Whoooaaaaaa" and

hacker's cough cackles coming from behind creaking doors.

'I'm getting the willies just thinking about it.'

Staff at Barry's had high hopes of a cushy day off because of the security alert, however these were soon dashed when a bus load of children broke down nearby, meaning people actually ventured into the park, if only to get out of the rain.

'F**k sake,' lamented three sibling staff members, Barry, Sam and Hugh Sments. 'We were totally just about to skive off and go the Harbour Bar and get pished. And we would have gotten away with it too if it hadn't been for those pesky kids.'

David Attenborough to film Blue Bag Planet documentary in Norn Iron

Following the success of *Planet Earth II*, naturalist David Attenborough has decided to update his *Blue Planet* series by visiting one of the most inhospitable places on earth – Northern Ireland.

Billed as the television event of the year, *Blue Bag Planet* will follow an indigenous species known as the Funnel-drinking Spide as it crosses treacherous mud plains in Mallusk and Magherafelt to reach the car parks of Cookstown and Carryduff, foraging for chips and Buckfast to sustain the herd.

BBC NI spokesman Colin Glen told us, 'The Funnel-drinking Spides are fascinating but we don't know much about them, as their aggressive nature makes it nearly impossible to get close without getting a boot up the hole and all your camera equipment nicked.

'Should David get among them, it'll make mucking around on the jungle floor with gorillas look like a day collecting butterflies at Antrim Road Waterworks.'

The crew are also hoping to get a glimpse of an even rarer beast, the Spide's mate – the lesser-spotted Millie.

'Naturally nocturnal and masters of camouflage, Millies blend into the background at the first sign of trouble,' Colin explained. 'However, they can be brash and loud if provoked. Spotting one is a possibility, what with all the new technology and alcoholic beverages at our disposal. We plan to entice them into the open by leaving bottles of WKD Blue near our hide.

'The ultimate would be to capture their notorious mating ritual, described as one of the most savage acts in the natural world. It usually takes place following a late-night illegal rave on the outskirts of Dunmurry and afterwards she eats him.'

The documentary-makers are understood to want filming to start as soon as possible, before the Spides and Millies move south to Millisle for the winter.

Northern Ireland hit with massive Tube strike

Despite not even having an underground rail network, Northern Ireland has been hit with a countrywide tube strike today as arseholes across the Province skived off work and angrily demanded a pay rise.

'Unlike our London comrades, who sadly cancelled their own strike today, we can't stop NI's transport system in its tracks by refusing to work,' said Ed Melter from the NI Union of Tubes. 'However we can bring the country to a standstill by being a right pain in the hole at every opportunity!

'Accordingly, our members are going to spend today trying to board packed trains before other passengers get off, using multiple bank cards at busy ATMs and nonchalantly buying scratch cards and Lotto Quick Picks at 8 a.m. when everyone else is rushing to get to work and just wants change for the bus!'

The strike will be supported by all fifty thousand members of the Northern Ireland Association of Tube Drivers.

'Not to be confused with our English counterparts, who actually drive underground trains, we drive cars,' explained local member, Joe Coach, 'except like absolute tubes!'

As a result, Northern Ireland's roads have come to a standstill today, with frustrated road users stuck behind people who insist on stopping at empty roundabouts, driving 10 mph under the speed limit on empty roads and slowly taking corners as if they are piloting an eighteen-wheeler – and not a Nissan Micra.

However one man we spoke to remained unfazed by the strike action. 'It sounds like just a normal day in Northern Ireland, tbh!' said Belfast man, Pastie McKeever. 'So I wouldn't be giving in to any of their demands.

'Unless they are looking a good boot up the hole,' he added.

Donegal named 'world's coolest place' following National Geographic blunder

Derry wans are pure raging according to reports, following the bizarre news that the place over the border they go to for dodgy diesel and pokes has been named one of the 'coolest' places in the entire world to visit.

'Your hole it is!' said Ralph Mullan, a twenty-seven-year-old retired painter and decorator from Creggan. 'I was down in Culdaff last week and Donegal wans still turn their jeans up and think dootsy checked shirts are the height of fashion!

'The men are just as bad,' he added.

National Geographic, who published the list, admitted that they 'made a whole balls of it' and that a simple communication mix-up had led to Donegal's inclusion.

'Ah FFS! We meant "coldest", not "coolest"!!' said *National Geographic* editor, Sally Bofey, earlier. 'The place would freeze the hole off you sure. Even dead warm-sounding towns like Ramelton and Burnfoot would f**king founder you.

'Although their Turkish Delights *are* far nicer,' she admitted.

The news has been confirmed by *Star Wars* actor Mark Hamill, who recently spent some time in Malin Head filming the latest instalment in the saga.

'I hadn't a clue what anyone was going on about,' admitted the sixty-five-year-old Luke Skywalker star. 'People kept asking me if I wanted a "can of mineral" or a "special of football" or some shite. My head was fried listening to them.

'So we would sneak out and head to Derry instead,' he revealed. 'We'd hit the Ice Wharf for a rake of cheap JD & Coke and then rock up to Da Vinci's to shift a coupla birds.

'Sadly Jedi mind tricks don't work on Derry weemin though,' he added. 'So I didn't get me hole.

'But on the plus side I got some cracker photos of the Peace Bridge!'

Northern Ireland 'not at centre of the universe', discover scientists

The world of science has been turned on its head by the findings of a new study conducted by scientists at Caledon Institute of Technology, better known as Caltech.

The County Tyrone boffins have apparently spent the last few months observing the movement of things called planets, and have come to the shocking conclusion that they do not, as previously thought, revolve around Northern Ireland.

'It turns out our preoccupation with all things local may not be entirely correct,' says Professor Brian Fox from Caltech's Astronomy Department. 'There may indeed be other stuff going on beyond our borders, things that may also have an impact on our planet.'

The news will come as a shock to the Province's parish-pump politicians and paramilitaries who are so intent on maintaining our navel-gazing focus.

'It is easy to forget that our continual petty squabbles over place names and symbolism pale into insignificance when we look at events on a global scale,' Fox explains. 'The scenes in Aleppo show us the terrible consequences of sectarian strife, and we should be grateful that we seem to be moving on from our own conflict.

'However they should also remind us that there are people, usually themuns, who would like nothing better than to drag us back into that kind of shite.'

Politicians here briefly removed their heads from their own arses to react predictably to the news, demanding that the report should be translated into Irish and Ulster-Scots before they'd give it due consideration.

10 last-minute Norn Iron gift ideas, probably for people you don't like

Once again *The Ulster Fry* consumer experts have been out scouring the shops for the best gifts available. There's something for everyone here.

1. Hipster Action Man............................

With realistic beard and an extravagant collection of tattoos, Hipster Action Man is the ultimate retro gift for the irritating fashionista in your life. Comes complete with oversized glasses, a small collection of exclusive craft beers and a ridiculously old-fashioned bike.

2. Buzz Shiteyear ....

This has been a year to forget, and Buzz will help you to remember what it is that you're meant to forget. Only £20.16 from all good toy shops.

3. Jimmy NES8BIT ....

Enjoy a feast of retro gaming in the company of international superstar James Nesbitt, with games including Street Fighter, Street Arguer, and Street You're My Best Mate, So Ye Are, Mucker.

4. County Tyrone Train Set...

Relive the thrill of a train ride in County Tyrone with Hornby's latest set. May not contain trains.

5. Go For Boke ....

The ultimate drinking game! Race your friends around the board collecting shots and see who can be first to make it to the porcelain throne room for a face-down visit.

6. Pamela Ballatwine...

One for those weird people who buy their pets presents, Pamela Ballatwine is the only celebrity-endorsed yarn wool-based plaything for cats. Made entirely from Pamela's hair, lovingly collected from the floor of the hairdressers by a team of dedicated stalkers.

THE NEW MUST HAVE CAT TOY THIS XMAS
PAMELA BALLATWINE

7. Hatchimlas...

Based on Hatchimals, 'Toy of the Year' Hatchimlas allow you to collect all your favourite local politicians. You don't know which MLA you'll get when you buy one, so we can expect much swapping in the playground after Christmas as kids try to trade Arlene Foster for Gerry Kelly. Like their namesakes, these yokes have sold out everywhere.

8. Little Tikes Black Taxi Playset...

Everything you need for a taxi tour of Belfast – complete with paramilitary record, a selection of utterly unbiased commentaries, a range of tattoos and a bootful of dodgy cigarettes.

LITTLE TIKES TAXI TOUR

9. Speak and Spell, Norn Iron Edition...

An educational toy that's fun for all the family. Master all those hard-to-spell words…

10. Lego Stormont...

Build it, have a minor crisis, dismantle it, build it again. Repeat every six months.

Craigavon man who went for tinfoil added to Queen's New Year honours list

A dad who left home today in a desperate Christmas Day search for turkey foil has been added to the Queen's New Year's Honours list.

Forty-six-year-old Willy Jumper, a half-civil servant from Craigavon, was alerted to the alarming shortage of Bacofoil at his home at around 10.30 a.m. this morning, sparking an heroic two-hour ordeal that took him to four neighbours' houses, five corner shops and two petrol stations, before he eventually struck gold, or aluminium to be precise, at a nearby eatery.

'I totally forgot how big my bird was!' explained Jumper afterwards. 'So when she squared up to me and said, "You better go and get foil now for this turkey!", I shit meself and pulled me coat on!

'I would have taken the car,' he continued, 'but it was nearly 11 a.m. and I'd been drinking a good four hours already … so I had to hoof it!

'Eventually I was able to explain my dilemma to some nice Asian people who were offloading stuff behind a Chinese takeaway,' he continued, 'by drawing tinfoil and turkey shapes in the air with my finger and talking really slowly.

'Thankfully they understood me – especially the doll with the Lurgan accent!'

This is not the first time a Christmas Day emergency has resulted in a prestigious award. In 2008, thirty-two-year-old

mother Brandy-Ann Baileys was awarded a CBE for finding a twelve-pack of AA batteries before her kids lost the plot.

'A devoted parent will drive a *real* car around the country for hours searching for batteries, so that their child can drive a toy car around the kitchen table for about two minutes before getting bored and doing something else,' confirmed leading child psychologist, Wayne Hayder.

'It's actually a good boot up the hole they need,' he confirmed.

Workplace violence erupts in row over who had quietest Christmas

Reports are coming in that heated workplace debates over who had the quietest Christmas are turning violent.

'Up and down the country grey-faced office workers are trying to outdo each other about who had the most boring time off,' says commander of the PSNI Riot Squad, Walter Cannon.

'These things start innocently enough. Someone says, "How was your Christmas?" and is told "Aye, quiet enough," but pretty soon someone takes it too far and all hell breaks loose.'

The warning comes after police were called to deal with disturbances at the headquarters of a major local

bank. 'It was mayhem,' we were told by an eyewitness. 'I just happened to mention that it'd been a quiet Christmas, then someone else claimed they hadn't left the house at all.

'Next thing, yer big man from the mortgage department leaps in shouting about how his had been the quietest Christmas as he hadn't even left his living room. Then everyone jumped in!'

An officer at the scene confirmed that several serious back-stabbings had taken place during the altercation, and that the riot squad were still dealing with passive-aggressive remarks being lobbed around the office.

'We are now trying to ID the woman who threw serious dirty looks at her colleagues this morning to start this madness,' confirmed officer Neil Norr. 'However, our photofit artists have had little success as she has about forty faces according to co-workers.'

Meanwhile bomb-disposal experts have been called to an accountant's office in Lisburn to deal with a suspected booby-trapped photocopier.

One man was taken away for questioning but has vowed to stay silent until 5 January in a final bid to win the quietest Christmas award.

The Ulster Fry

Eggs

Fury as vandals change Holywood town sign

People in Holywood are described as 'quite cross' today after vandals doctored one of the town's iconic name signs to read 'Holewood'.

The pranksters appear to have been inspired by events in California, after the famous sign on the Hollywood hills was changed to Hollyweed on New Year's Eve.

Police in the North Down town say that the crime has all the hallmarks of a politically-motivated attack.

'It's clearly a message from our neighbours in Bangor,' we were told by PSNI Sergeant Kostas Coffey. 'People here aren't too happy that they scooped that "Town most up its own hole" award last year, as we'd been working really hard at being up ours, and those Bangor ones love rubbing it in at every opportunity.

'We haven't made any arrests yet, but we reckon it's the same shadowy group who changed the sign on the Maypole to MyHole back in November.'

Local shopkeeper Tiffany Lamp-Shayde told us that she was distraught when she heard about the attack. 'I'm distraught,' she said. 'I was just saying to my sister Crystal that the town had really bounced back after missing out on that prize. Then this happens – it's enough to drive you to prosecco.'

Retired pensioner Sullivan Upper revealed that he was ready to take the law into his own hands. 'They've crossed a line here,' he argued. 'I'm as far up my own hole as the next man, and I won't have those plebs saying otherwise. I fully intend to make a citizen's arrest at some point, should the need arise.'

A spokesman for Bangor denied that they were involved in the attack.

'It was New Year's Day, FFS,' he told us, 'We were all playing golf or down at the yacht club eating artisan cheeses and talking about Range Rovers. It must have been those oiks from Cultra.'

Buck-mad overtaker to be two cars ahead at next roundabout, confirm Road Service

The NI Road Service has confirmed that the ejjit who nearly killed you, himself and everyone on an oncoming bus whilst overtaking you at around 127 mph will be about 23 feet ahead of you at the next roundabout.

The news has been gleefully welcomed by everyone, except the driver himself, who is now reportedly looking in his rear-view mirror, giving you a fierce dirty look and wondering if you are really the same car.

'We can confirm that is the boy who nearly ran you off the road a while ago because 78 mph wasn't fast enough,' said Cara Nodden-Gere from the Roundabout Inspection Unit. 'And that he's now only 21 feet behind you, cos the girl behind you just moved forward a wee bit.'

However the news has been slammed by the Irish Association of Impatient Motorists Angrily Driving In Cars With a Deathwish (IAMADICWAD), who say their man would now be 'miles ahead', if he'd not got stuck behind a lorry. 'He'd have got around the hur if it wasn't for the frustratingly long stretches of straight road and safe, passing spots that prevented him from making our signature move,' said IAMADICWAD spokesman Paddy Subaru.

'He'll blast him shortly though,' he boasted. 'There are a couple of long, winding roads ahead with no oncoming visibility that are perfect for overtaking multiple cars at once whilst simultaneously shrinking the arseholes of nearby motorists to the size of a neutron.'

The news has been welcomed by the Ulster Regiment of Sizeable Lorry Owners (URSLO) spokesperson Aideen Wheeler. 'Our work transporting goods to supermarkets, hospitals and factories pales into insignificance for the average impatient driver. We look forward to working closely alongside them – especially whilst hurtling towards oncoming traffic at 80 mph!'

'We fully understand that your man is in a wile hurry,' she added. 'No one wants to be late for a speed awareness course.'

WE'RE HAVING TWINS

Beyoncé 'absolutely raging' with George Clooney, admits pal Barra Best

Popstar Beyoncé, who recently got news at the Ulster Hospital that she had two buns in the oven, is reportedly 'pure snapping' at George Clooney and his wife Amal for 'blatantly copying' her and her husband, according to Jay Z's best mucker, BBCNI weatherman Barra Best.

Clooney, who lives with his glamorous wife in a semi-detached in Doagh, is said to have taken his missus to Whiteabbey Hospital for a 'wee check-up' yesterday, after growing increasingly concerned that she'd spent several mornings in a row boking into a bin.

It was there they discovered they too were having twins.

'Bey is currently feeling a high-pressure front building up in her temporal lobes,' Barra explained. 'As that rage lingers we'll see a long period of tears, followed by occasional snotters and scattered outbursts of gurning.

'After that we'll see a huge cold front develop!'

Tensions are indeed at all-time high between the rival power couples, eclipsing the war of words that broke out last month when Jay Z's gig upstairs in The Errigle got reviewed in the *Belfast Telegraph*, whilst George's latest movie premiere only got picked up by the *Andytown News*.

'There will be some fierce dirty looks fired out this weekend down in Castlecourt!' revealed Clooney's good pal, Malachi Cush. 'I hear they are both after the same McLaren Double Dreamcatcher buggy in Argos … and apparently there's only wan left!

'God forbid they end up trying on maternity wear in H&M at the same time. There'll be blue murder!'

Following the news of twins, it's rumoured that Jay Z has upgraded the lyrics of his most famous track to now include 999 problems.

However Beyoncé's publicist has dismissed this report, insisting that her husband 'doesn't do a f**king tap anyway'.

Northern Ireland's 7 most interesting car parks

No day out in Northern Ireland is complete without a visit to one of the many fascinating car parks that serve our towns and cities – but have you ever stopped to think about the amazing stories that lie behind them?

Hopefully not, but we've been doing our research …

1. Ards Shopping Centre.....................................

Opened by King George VI in 1963, Ards Shopping Centre was the first building in Northern Ireland to include two-way doors. The car park itself was designed by top architect Frank Lloyd Wright, who included a unique 'shit road layout' to ensure that it would be impossible to find a space at any time of the day or night.

2. Crescent Link Retail Park, Derry/Londonderry ....

A non-existent one-way system and a cunningly placed zebra crossing make this the Hotel California of the car park world – you can check in any time you like, but you can never leave. King James I parked his army here during the Siege of Derry, which is why he lost.

3. The one by the play park, Plumbridge......................

With space for an incredible seven vehicles, this car park is a must-see destination for *Game of Thrones* fans as it features in season 3, episode 2, as the place where Jon Snow has a nasty fall off the swings. Conveniently situated across from Pinkerton's shap, it's also a great spot to enjoy a poke on a Sunday afternoon.

4. The King's Stables, Armagh ....

Another great place for a poke, as apparently this is one of Northern Ireland's top spots for doggers. *The Ulster Fry* had to Google 'Best places for dogging in Northern Ireland' whilst researching this piece, resulting in some trouble with Mrs Ulster Fry. Anyone conducting similar research would be advised to delete their search history.

5. Victoria Square, Belfast ....

According to Guinness World Records, this is the world's most expensive car park, costing an incredible £342 for fifteen minutes. Once inside, your car will be kept warm by an impressively pointless heating system which ensures sub-tropical temperatures all year round – unlike inside the centre itself, which is like a Siberian wind tunnel even in July.

6. Bloomfield Shopping Centre ....

A complete hell hole, described by the magazine *Car Park Monthly* as having been 'designed by a blind dog having a shite'. Visitors should set aside at least fourteen hours for any trip to allow time to drive round and round before discovering that it's virtually impossible to get back out again. There's f**k all interesting about it, although it's probably where Jamie Dornan did something boring in an episode of *The Fall*.

7. The one beside the electric toilets, Ballywalter...

More a patch of grass than a car park, tourists can nevertheless abandon their vehicle here if they're early enough, allowing them to spend the day secure in the knowledge that they're close to both the toilets and the beach. Kanye West lists this as his favourite place on the Ards Peninsula for a coort.

Have we missed any out?
Please don't tell us as we don't care.

Trump buys Scrabo Tower ahead of historic NI visit

Following an invite to visit Northern Ireland, *The Ulster Fry* has learned that Donald Trump is to expand his portfolio of eponymous real-estate landmarks by buying Scrabo Tower in County Down.

'We've accepted an offer from Mr Trump and it's worth a clean fortune!' revealed former owner, Newton Ards. 'He asked me how much I was looking so I just pulled a massive number out of my hole, for the craic. I nearly shit a brick when he said, "Aye, that's grand hi, the Mexicans are paying for it anyway!" He's off his rocker!'

Trump's historic visit to Ulster remains shrouded in mystery, but our source at the White House did reveal some exclusive details of his trip.

'President Trump reckons he can really help the Northern Ireland peace process!' revealed White House aide, Dick Wallbasher. 'Not only is he a die-hard republican, but he's got decades of experience as an orange man … so he's ideally qualified to bring both sides together!'

'He's inviting all the Northern Ireland politicians out for dinner, drinks and a bitta craic,' he continued.

'We haven't finalised a venue yet,' he admitted. 'The Spaniard seems too foreign. The Merchant sounds like it'll be full of immigrants and he's not big into that whole Europa craic … but the Northern Whig, Fibber Magee and Whites Tavern caught his eye!'

It is then expected that President Trump will head west of the Bann, taking the Ulsterbus 212 to Derry. 'Aye, he heard they have a border with "Mexico" and a big massive wall that was used for keeping people out.'

Arlene Foster is also planning on bringing the President to Fermanagh, where she said Mr Trump can expect 'a very warm welcome' at an official state banquet in a local chicken shed.

'We're more shit than you,' Craigavon tells Strabane

Residents in crap towns and villages across Northern Ireland have reacted angrily to a report that labelled Strabane as being full of 'skint, vodka-swilling gamblers'.

'How come they get all the credit?' was the bemused reaction of Craigavon native Rhonda Bout when we told her the news. 'Craigavon is way more shit than Strabane, and yet they get the headlines. They're up their own holes, so they are.'

Larne resident Brian Ferry was also furious. 'We've spent years building our hard-earned reputation as a complete dump, then these Johnny-come-latelys land in and take all the plaudits. And what about Carrick? It's an absolute hellhole, and it doesn't even get a mention. Themuns get everything.'

Portrush man Barry O'Musement also hit out at the report. 'It's a real slap in the face for our town,' he said. 'They're clearly trying to muscle in on our tourist trade, but people should remember that if they want to swill vodka and gamble, Portrush is the place to do it.'

In Hillsborough, local DUP councillor Drew Abelheat-Incentive was equally scathing. 'It ignores the fact that even posh places like ours can be shit. We're just shit in a different, more refined way, proving that you can polish a turd.'

However the Mayor of Derry and Strabane Council has rejected criticism of the Tyrone town.

'These people in other towns need to take a long, hard look at themselves,' she told us. 'Places like Strabane don't just become shit overnight. It's taken decades of chronic underfunding to earn this accolade, so they needn't think they can just nip in at the last minute and steal our glory.'

No one from Strabane was available for comment as they don't have any mobile phone signal.

6 reasons why petrol stations are a pain in the hole

Petrol stations are really f**king annoying – this is a fact.

They are all the more annoying because, unlike other annoying shops that sell nothing but candles and signs that say 'Live, Love, Life', you have no choice but to go to them, if you have a car.

We've conducted an in-depth survey of a member of the public to see what it is that makes them so annoying. Here are the results.

1. People who park at the pumps for ages.

Let's get this one out of the way early. You've paid for your petrol, you're back in your car. There is no need to sit for half an hour doing your hair or checking your phone. Just drive out of the way and let someone else in. It's called basic f**king manners.

2. They sell far too much stuff these days.

You've got your fuel, you're gonna get a can of coke or something, but you end up wandering round and round for twenty minutes trying to find the fridge, which they've moved to the very back just to force you to wander round the ginormous shop where you might suddenly think, 'Oh, I need dog food', then you remember you don't have a dog.

3. People who do their entire weekly shop in them.

This is a direct result of number 2. Having found the fridge you go up to pay and there's some auld doll in front of you with one of those mini trolleys piled to the ceiling with bog roll and Pedigree Chum. She's just landed at the till, her purse is in the car, and it's parked at a pump.

4. The state of the toilets.

You're busting for a slash on the drive from Belfast to Derry or Belfast to London (depending on who painted over the sign), so you stop at a garage. When you get into the bog the previous occupant has somehow crapped everywhere apart from in the bowl, while simultaneously flooding the floor with pish. WHAT IS WRONG WITH PEOPLE? Do they do this at home?

5. They make you pay for air.

In the old days they had a compressor out the back attached to an air line, and it was free. Now it's 20p because they're tight bastards, apart from the Applegreen Services on the motorway, so I drive there for badness.

6. The big signs they place on the pavement.

It's a petrol station – it requires cars to get both in and out. Why place massive signs at the exit so you can't see the traffic? We know you do two big things of milk for £2 – all petrol stations do two big things of milk for £2 – but we don't need 8 feet signs blowing about in the wind to tell us.

Apart from all these things they're great, now sort it out, petrol stations.

Fury as slightly higher bar replaces Ponderosa as Ireland's highest pub

There was sporadic violence on the Glenshane Pass today after locals awoke to find that the famous Ponderosa Bar had been stripped of its 'Highest Pub in Ireland' title by a new establishment built a few hundred yards further up the hillside.

It is understood that the new pub, called The High Chaparral, was erected overnight by cowboy builders working for an English pub chain, in a move condemned by one Glenshane resident as 'Pure sleekit'.

News of the surprising erection soon spread across the district, and an angry mob spent several hours climbing the Magherafelt side of the pass, before launching an exhausted protest at the summit.

Violence followed with reports that at least one speed-camera van had been shouted at and a number of sheep overturned, blocking traffic heading in the direction of Draperstown.

Politicians in the area are appealing for calm after what has been described by police sources as 'a wile handlin".

'These are the worst scenes of recreational rural rioting I've seen on the Glenshane since Jamesies Centra stopped selling beef sausage rolls in 1998,' we were told by Superintendent Tamlaght O'Crilly. 'Everyone involved needs to catch themselves on – or we might have to leave the station.'

Meanwhile a bar in West Belfast, which has also claimed to be the 'highest pub in the country', has been disqualified from the competition after it was pointed out that it's based on how far above sea level the establishment is – not how frequently regulars nip into the bogs to snort coke off the toilet cistern.

South Armagh lettuce smuggling operation raided by PSNI

As the world vegetable shortage continues to bite, police on both sides of the border have made arrests after a 'significant lettuce cache' was uncovered on a farm outside Forkhill in South Armagh.

It is believed that smugglers with links to the Republican movement have shifted tactics in recent weeks, moving away from diesel laundering towards the lucrative trade in illicit vegetables.

'We received intelligence that indicated that a major vegetable distribution network was operating in the area,' said Superintendent

Bryce Berg of the PSNI. 'Acting on this information, our officers conducted raids on properties in the South Armagh area. Six suspects have been arrested, and fourteen tonnes of laundered lettuce seized along with a number of viable cucumbers.'

Among those in custody is Tobias 'Spud' Murphy, a well-known smuggler who security sources claim has been dealing in illegal potatoes since the 1970s. Former chief Shinner Gerry Adams has leapt to Mr Murphy's defence, telling reporters that 'Tobias is a good Republican' and condemning the operation as 'indicative of the "hard border" mentality we will face in a post-Brexit Ireland'.

Authorities on both sides of the border are so determined to stamp out vegetable smuggling that they've introduced coloured dyes into salad and vegetables, similar to those added to diesel.

At the time of writing over fifty cars suspected of being full of red or green cabbage had been impounded at the Monaghan border.

Royal Mint launch separate 'Pound' coin for Northern Ireland

The Head Spokesminter of the Royal Mint announced today that the newly-launched £1 coin, much lauded for being more secure, would not be legal tender in Northern Ireland until an Executive is formed.

'The launch of the new coin was a momentous day for us,' said Bob Pounder, 'but we couldn't risk damaging its reputation in the financial markets. We had no choice but to mint a different coin to allow for the unique circumstances in NI. After many long minutes of consultation with our Special Advisers, we agreed that the £1.60 coin was the ideal solution!'

The 'RHI Pound' operates in much the same way as the £1 coin in Britain, however it is considered less durable due to it being constructed almost entirely from wood pellets. 'The metals in the £1 coin are too expensive, we just couldn't take the risk of using them in Northern Ireland right now. It's easier to just paint the coins gold,' Mr Pounder added.

Conleth Punt, a greengrocer from Castlerock, said, 'Sure, if you spend yer pound canny enough in NI, these days you get a quid sixty back anyway, so I guess it makes sense.'

We sought comment from Northern Ireland's Finance Minister for his opinion on this currency snub, but discovered that there isn't one.

However, most MLAs are delighted at the news. 'Coupled with our pay rise, this means we'll be raking it in for doing feck all,' West Tyrone representative Jimmy Cash told us as he changed out of his pyjamas this afternoon.

French car manufacturers to rebrand for Northern Ireland motorists

French car companies have finally woken up to the fact that many people here struggle to pronounce their names, and are to undergo complete rebrands to suit the Northern Irish consumer.

According to Parisian motoring journalist Sylvestre Lecat, the change was inevitable.

'May wee,' he told us, 'vous est totally unable to say les French woords. We have been knowing of this pour years. By changing of the names the cars de la France weel get un grande sales boost.'

The Northern Ireland Culchie Federation, an umbrella group for rural dwellers here, has welcomed the move.

'100 per cent, hi. 100 per cent,' said NICF spokesman Matty Ferguson. 'Sure fur now when we chat about the Renalt S-Pace, the Poojoe Wan-Oh-Sax and the Sitrin Extra Pickassa, folk will know what we're bletherin' about, so they will, hi, so they will.'

Other motor manufacturers are believed to be considering similar moves, with plans underway for the launch of the Voltswagan, Hayundee and Fate brands later this year.

However Spanish car giants SEAT have said they can't be arsed changing the spelling and are just going to pronounce their name seat like everyone else.

Hacking Smart TVs 'completely pointless in Northern Ireland' admits CIA

Attempts by the US Central Intelligence Agency to monitor fundamentalist groups in Northern Ireland by hacking so-called 'Smart' devices such as TVs and phones have failed miserably, security sources have revealed.

'Basically this involves accessing the device's microphone or camera,' says top US spymaster Felix Lighter, 'but to be honest when we tried it on you lot we hadn't a clue what anyone was saying.'

An early attempt to infiltrate the Coalisland branch of Islamic State was a catastrophic failure. 'We managed to hack into the leader's TV set,' he says, 'but ended up in a fruitless search for a terrorist commander called Su'Kine Dei'Sel and his henchman Qu'are Al Bai, and what we thought was a developing turf war with a rival cell was in reality just an argument about turf.'

Similar efforts to hack criminal gangs elsewhere in the country also failed.

'The Limavady Yakuza and the Portballintrae Triads were impossible to understand,' says

Lighter. 'We thought we were onto a major drugs cartel but it turns out every time we thought they said *heroin* they actually said *hoagherin*', and the "big heroin ship" their leader was expecting was just a particularly smelly shite. It wasn't pleasant when our agents burst in on him, I'll tell ye.'

However there have been some successes.

'After all our efforts it turned out to be easy enough to find all your fundamentalist nutters,' explains Lighter. 'Instead of hacking TVs you only had to turn them on and watch the election results.'

Storm Doris blows Isle of Man north to form land bridge to Scotland

Ferry operators in Larne and Belfast are engaged in crisis meetings this evening after the Isle of Man broke free of its moorings in high winds and drifted north, before becoming wedged between Northern Ireland and Scotland.

BREAKING NEWS
ISLE OF MAN BREAKS ANCHOR - NOW STUCK OFF ARDS PENINSULA

Image courtesy of NISA
(The shop, not the space agency)

The problems began this morning after a rope tethering the cat-infested island to the bottom of the Irish Sea was severed by a passing Russian submarine. Fishermen attempted to anchor it back in place using nets but by then it had already drifted over 40 miles and the situation was hopeless.

Eyewitness Billy Halbert told us what he saw as it passed the Ards Peninsula. 'I was looking

out my kitchen window to see if the postman had been and the next thing I saw this huge lump floating past out at sea.

'At first I thought nothing of it,' he continued, 'but then I noticed it had a wee flag with three legs on it, and I realised that it wasn't Nolan taking swimming lessons – it had to be an accidentally dislocated landmass that would, in all likelihood, end up wedged between here and Wigtownshire.'

Engineers and geologists were immediately called to the scene in the hope of loosening the Manx island, but despite slootering no less than 47 tonnes of butter around the edges it remained firmly lodged in place.

'We may as well make the best of it,' said bridges expert Sydney Harbour. 'Instead of towing it back, we'll build a road onto it and slash the cost of getting to Scotland.'

With the Assembly suspended there has yet to be a response from Stormont, but it is understood that the main political parties have already dispatched canvassers to the former island to see if the new voters will be usuns or themuns.

Giant's Causeway built by National Trust, says National Trust

The National Trust has laid centuries of conjecture to rest by announcing that they built the Giant's Causeway, and that anyone who fancies a dander round it should pay handsomely for the privilege.

'People used to think that a giant built it, or that it was formed in the great flood out of the Bible,' says Trust spokesman Brock Formation. 'There were even folk who claimed it was formed by some kind of volcanic eruption. I mean, how ridiculous is that? Now we can finally set the record straight!

'Our archaeologists have discovered that it was actually constructed by Stone Age National Trust volunteers to create a visitor experience for prehistoric tourists.

'We've uncovered evidence of a primitive car park close to the Causeway itself,' he revealed. 'There's even a rudimentary toilet facility with urinals labelled "Ye Olde Armitage Shanks" and bog roll made of slabs of slate.'

Most convincingly of all, a prehistoric gift shop has also been found. 'It sold all kind of ancient tourist tat,' we were told. 'Wooden clubs decorated with the National Trust symbol, souvenir stationery like spear sharpeners and stone tablet notepads, even a T-shirt that says "My ancestors went to the Giant's Causeway and all I got was this lousy mammoth skin".'

As a result of the discovery, the attraction will now be renamed The Giant's Car Park, but anyone wishing to visit is advised to arrange a substantial bank loan in advance as ticket prices are likely to rise.

'It costs a fortune keeping half the Causeway closed,' explains Formation, 'and we need to preserve the National Trust for future generations.'

Holylands students set for tea and quiet reflection following booze ban

Students have cancelled St Patrick's Day plans in the Holylands it has emerged, following the news that nearby off-licences would close for a few hours tomorrow to help stop anti-social behaviour.

'Ack, no way! We were pure up for going clean mental too!' said twenty-two-year-old Carmel Street, 'but fair play to the crafty hurs, they've stopped us dead in our tracks. We're just gonna sit in now instead … maybe clean the house and catch up on our assignments, etc.!'

Her housemate Phil Jotter reluctantly agreed. 'I was planning to bate two litres of Buckfast into me and then sprint up and down our street in acid-green glittery hot pants, kicking over wheelie bins and screaming "Yeeeeooooo",' he revealed. 'But that's out the window now, fer fuck's sake …

'I'll just stick the kettle on and do some exam revision instead!' he sighed.

Officer Dan Steelie of the PSNI's Zero-Craic Enforcement Division is confident the plan will work despite the obvious criticism that students can easily get around it by simply buying a carry-out tonight instead.

'NI students are incapable of having unopened drink lying around the house overnight!' he explained. 'They might be able to ignore the call of the blue bag for a few hours … but by 10 p.m. they'll be getting wired into it 100 per cent! There won't be a drop left by morning!'

The scheme has also come under fire from social media observers, who have pointed out that simply walking to an off-licence up the road is another obvious workaround.

'True …' revealed a Students' Union spokesman, 'but we couldn't be arsed!'

10 dull Norn Iron things to do on a Sunday

Whilst the DUP don't like doing *anything* on a Sunday, in the real world Norn Iron folk love doing *stuff*. Here are our top picks.

1. Go out for Sunday Carvery ....

Show your family how much you love them by declaring that you couldn't be arsed cooking for them and pay someone else to do it instead. Bond with them over the agonising decision of turkey & ham or roast beef, before regretting your choice because theirs looks far nicer. Later rate the restaurant on TripAdvisor based on whether they had crayons or charged for blackcurrant squash.

2. Visit the seaside ....

Whilst Brian Kennedy may wistfully always wish he was in Carrickfergus, everyone who actually lives there wishes they *weren't*. Northern Ireland has a wide selection of similarly baltic seaside towns with world-class attractions, including poke vans, seesaws, ageing roller coasters and public toilets, some of which have them fancy 20p lock yokes on the door.

3. IKEA ....

It's Sunday morning. You wake to find your missus wearing that sexy underwear you like. Feeling frisky, you kiss her shoulder gently. She turns around and smiles at you and whispers something sexy like, 'Hey, lets go to IKEA today.' Overpowered by an insatiable lust to spend all of your wages, you rip on all your clothes and spend the entire day in beds with her. The

romance is almost ruined when she catches you eyeing up that SKÄNK in the kitchen department. Your explanation that it's 'just for throwing the spuds into' doesn't help matters.

4. Church/Mass ....

Northern Ireland is a society divided by religion. One half of the population *thinks* church is boring, whilst the other half openly admits it. Regardless of whether you go to church or Mass though, there can be little doubt that God truly is our Father – because every time you visit him he tells you the same story he did last week … and the week before.

5. Your local leisure centre ....

Whilst 'dropping the kids off at the pool' has become synonymous with having a shit, *actually* dropping the kids off at the pool has become synonymous with having a shit day. Car parking, several swim passes, new goggles for Sophie, money for the vending machines and the inevitable cries for post-swim ice cream … Yep, right about now you are looking at your bank balance wondering why you didn't just buck them into the sea at Carrickfergus. Still, at least your car doesn't smell like chlorine and wet dog… oh wait.

6. A jungle gym – with a hangover ....

Nothing says family bonding quite like the local custom of bucking three dozen strange kids into a heavily-padded, multicoloured detention centre, whilst their bored, hungover parents sit nearby drinking overpriced weak-ass tea hoping they will be left alone for an hour. For extra hangover points, freak out that a creepy man has kidnapped your missing child, then realise that they have merely had their face painted to look like Spider-Man. On leaving, cleverly distract Spider-Man with a Fruit Shoot whilst applying shoes.

7. Connswater Shopping Centre...

Situated in East Belfast, Connswater was recently voted one of NI's favourite locations for surviving a zombie apocalypse. Thrilled by the accolade, shoppers get into the spirit by shuffling about the centre in their pyjamas like the army of the undead. 'It's a great day out for the family,' revealed centre manager Argos Barrett. 'We've got one of those kiddy-ride machines that bobs up and down for sixty seconds for £1 … and our mezzanine food court has breathtaking views of the car park!'

8. Titanic Dock...

Impress friends and family with NI's rich engineering history by taking them to a big hole in the ground where they once built a boat that sank. Ponder the cultural heritage of the docklands for minutes on end, before quietly deciding it's f**king baltic and going to find a pub instead. Maybe they'll have a nice Sunday carvery…

9. Visit the in-laws ....

If you like cake, talking about the weather and in-depth discussions about healthcare, then visiting the in-laws is the perfect Sunday getaway. Get first-hand accounts on the shortcomings of your partner's siblings, all whilst educating your little angels about technology by hopelessly explaining why you can't pause or rewind granny's TV.

10. Drive out for ice cream ....

Why not bundle all your little bundles of joy into the car and hit the open road in search of something sweet and cold? For the real authentic experience, try passing a few actual ice-cream parlours in the hope of finding something even better, before getting hopelessly lost and then buying pokes from a petrol station instead.

Fury as passenger is ejected from Translink Goldliner service

There is widespread anger on social media today after a passenger was forcibly removed from the 238 Express service from Belfast to Newry.

In a virtual replay of what happened on a United Airlines flight yesterday, the incident occurred after the passenger, named locally as Justin Thyme, took his seat at the Europa terminus.

It is understood that around forty-five pensioners then boarded the bus, all of them returning to Hillsborough having travelled up on their free passes to 'get a quick coffee and maybe call into Marksies' earlier in the day.

Staff were then forced to make the difficult choice between leaving behind the paying customer or one of the pensioners. 'We decided on Mr Thyme,' said Translink spokeswoman Perpetua Pryce-Rise. 'To be honest we couldn't be arsed listening to thesuns moaning on Nolan the next morning.'

Police were called after Mr Thyme refused to budge and he was eventually removed and charged with resisting a ridiculous request.

'They made the right decision,' said seventy-five-year-old Wanda Moan from Annahilt. 'I was just saying to my friend Jean how we'd paid taxes our whole lives to get these free passes, even though they were introduced after we stopped paying taxes. These pesky paying passengers are always taking up our seats – you'd think they'd only allow people to pay outside peak times or something.'

Footage of the incident hasn't gone viral on social media as none of the witnesses can work a smartphone.

EXCLUSIVE
Fast & Furious 9 to be filmed in Northern Ireland

With their eighth globe-trotting instalment currently breaking box office records, Vin Diesel has confirmed that the next *Fast & Furious* movie will be shot in Northern Ireland.

'Toretto's crew is going back to basics!' revealed Diesel. 'Their cash is running out, so they'll be relying on their wits, instincts and ability to spot a clinker at the mid-Ulster auctions to get back on the road!'

Diesel's co-star Michelle Rodriguez has also spoken about the project. '*Fast 8* was all about spectacular car crashes and mind-blowing stunts,' she told us, 'so it's no surprise that most of us qualify for high-rate DLA now. One of the first scenes is a tense negotiation with John Mulholland over a Motability deal on a Skoda Octavia!

'Thon heated seats really help my sciatica!' she revealed.

Other cast members have already flown in for specialist NI driving training. 'We've been practising "donuts" on a road outside Aughnacloy,' revealed Tyrese Gibson. 'Apart from the fact it's a whole handlin' driving on the left, all the local wans call them something else. The hurs keep asking us to do "Gravy Rings", FFS!'

The identity of the main villain hasn't been confirmed yet, but sources indicate that a Dungannon Audi A4 driver who drives up Vin Diesel's hole between Castledawson and Dungiven will replace Jason Statham as the movie's antagonist.

'This boy is a proper hallion,' revealed Diesel. 'In one scene he's doing 110 mph trying to get past me. In another he's driving through a housing estate at 2 mph in case the speed bumps scratch his new alloys. Toretto's head is pure fried with him!

'And to make it worse, VOSA keep pulling me into the side of the road to stick a tube down my throat and test what sorta Diesel I *really* am!

'Ballbegs' he added.

The Fast, The Slow & The Wile Infuriating will begin shooting this summer.

44

Innovative Belfast barbershop to offer only haircuts

NO BEARD OIL NO CRAFT BEER NO MUSTACHE WAX NO PRIZE FIGHTING NO AXE SHAVES

The world of male grooming was turned on its head today, as one Belfast barbershop unveiled an audacious plan to simply cut men's hair without trying to pretend they are prize fighters, 1920s dockers, lumberjacks or Vikings.

Nick's Barbers on Queen Street shocked business experts by insisting that they won't be selling craft beer at the premises, or providing a range of arty magazines on woodwork, classic bicycle maintenance, artisan coffee grinding or obscure martial arts.

'We've got the Mirror, the Daily Star, yesterday's Belfast Telegraph and a copy of the Sunday Sport that someone else brought and left behind … swear!' revealed Nick McComb, the mastermind behind the initiative.

'Our concept is that you come in, read a paper, and when it's your turn, we ask you if you are heading anywhere on your holidays, what you do yourself and if ye head out the town much. We'll also drop in some small talk about sport, ask ye what team you support, etc.

'Then at the end, we show you the back of your head in the mirror, take a few quid off ye and shout, "Who's next there?"

'It's a really different approach but customers seem to like it,' he added. Some sceptics are not convinced though.

'I rode my penny-farthing down there the other day to buy some beard oil but I was aghast to discover they didn't sell any!' revealed local man, Thor Dohertysson.

'I thought I'd give them a go anyway, but I was disappointed to learn that they haven't bothered to paper the walls in fake brickwork pattern, hang any skateboards, samurai swords or knuckle-dusters on the ceiling, or provide a Nespresso machine for customers. I got up and walked out!

'Turns out all they do is cut your hair,' he moaned. 'Which is a shame, cos all I wanted was a haircut.'

The Ulster Fry Guide to Stereotypes

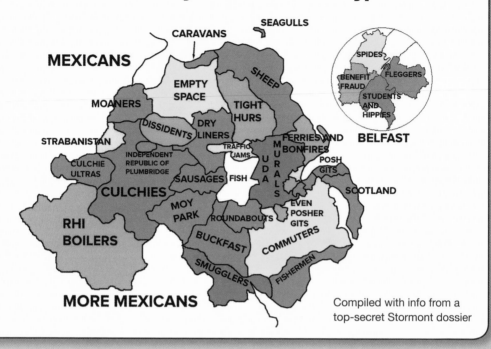

SEAGULLS

CARAVANS

MEXICANS

EMPTY SPACE

SHEEP

MOANERS

TIGHT HURS

STRABANISTAN

DISSIDENTS

DRY LINERS

TRAFFIC JAMS

FERRIES AND BONFIRES

M U R A L S

U D A

POSH GITS

CULCHIE ULTRAS

INDEPENDENT REPUBLIC OF PLUMBRIDGE

SAUSAGES

FISH

CULCHIES

MOY PARK

ROUNDABOUTS

EVEN POSHER GITS

SCOTLAND

RHI BOILERS

BUCKFAST

COMMUTERS

SMUGGLERS

FISHERMEN

MORE MEXICANS

SPIDES

BENEFIT FRAUD

FLEGGERS

STUDENTS AND HIPPIES

BELFAST

Compiled with info from a top-secret Stormont dossier

North Kilrea placed on high alert amid fears of Korea mix-up

The ruling council of North Kilrea has raised the region's security status to 'DEFCON Wan, hi' amid fears that US President Donald Trump may be preparing for military action in the area.

'We're taking the threat very seriously,' the President of the local Sheepdog Society, Jim Young-Wan told us, 'The citizens of the Democratic People's Republic of North Kilrea will not be intimidated by the sabre rattling of the Yankee devils.'

The rise in tension comes after local farmers carried out tests on what security experts described as 'intercontinental ballistic slurry tankers capable of delivering huge payloads of shite over several fields'. A further test followed a display of vintage tractors yesterday afternoon, but this one exploded prematurely, showering observers in pig dung.

The use of the powerful agricultural equipment has caused concern in South Kilrea, which has been backed by the USA in the long-running dispute with its communist neighbour. A message of support from President Trump was delivered to South Kilrean leader Sean-Joe Mahon this morning, although it understood that the Post Office is closed so he hasn't got it yet.

'We are prepared to act, and have sent a very powerful fleet to the area. Very powerful. We have the most powerful fleet in the world. USA, USA.' Mr Trump told journalists, 'It would be good if the Chinese would help, but if they won't, we will act alone.'

It is believed that Mr Trump was referring to the Golden Panda Chinese takeaway in Coleraine, which has traditionally supported North Kilrea by delivering battered chicken balls and curry chips to the area.

In a related and equally tenuous story the Marble Arch Caves complex has been closed after the US Airforce dropped the Mother of All Bombs on it yesterday morning. No one from the County Fermanagh branch of Islamic State is available for comment.

Fury after new Ballymena resident cuts grass on a Sunday

'I was pretty sure he was one of us,' was the most common reaction in Ballymena this evening after a man described locally as a 'blow-in' was observed mowing his front lawn on the Lord's Day.

It is understood that thirty-four-year-old Steven Walsh took his Qualcast corded rotary lawnmower from his shed at 3.30 p.m., and proceeded to brazenly cut his grass, despite

this being against the Fourth Commandment.

'I wasn't too sure of him when he moved in,' says fellow Queen's Drive resident Herbert Robinson. 'I mean, you can't tell with a name like that, but now I'm pretty sure he's one of themuns.'

However local themun Fintan O'Neill disagrees. 'I've never seen him doing anything stereotypically "usuns",' he claimed. 'I mean, he's never in the pub on a Sunday, and I've never seen him wearing any O'Neill's sportswear. I've also heard he spells his name with a "v" rather than a "ph", which is a surefire sign of the heretic.'

The confusion has since spread to neighbouring estates, where several residents took advantage of the sound of Mr Walsh's lawnmower to hoke out their power tools.

'I'm always worried about what the neighbours will think,' we were told by one gardener. 'As soon as I heard him start up I was out the back with the chainsaw, cutting everything in sight.'

The PSNI have confirmed that they have had several reports of illegal Sunday gardening, and are preparing a report for the Director of Ridiculous Prosecutions.

Fury as Newtownstewart removes the word Easter from its name

There was outrage in the sleepy County Tyrone town of Newtownstewart today after it emerged that the National Trust had removed the letters of the word Easter from its road sign.

The wanton act of vandalism was spotted by a motorist who missed his turn-off after thinking he was somewhere called Nwtownwt, and ended up driving on to Strabane. 'That was the worst thing about it, to be honest,' he told us. 'No one should accidentally end up in Strabane.'

The driver duly raised the alarm, and a crowd of angry residents gathered in the town centre where a reporter from the *Daily Telegraph* told them that the National Trust was to blame.

The Ulster Fry understands that the townsfolk considered marching to the nearest Trust property in protest, but that turned out to be Gray's Printers in Strabane and no one wanted to go. After a discussion, they set fire to some of that nice National Trust soap instead.

The Archbishop of Canterbury soon waded into the argument. 'This is a blatant attempt to airbrush our Christian Heritage from things by removing the letters of Easter in them,' he told the BBC. 'Weather forecasters will be talking about Southly winds instead of Southeasterly – even the forecasters will soon be called "weather forcs".'

The furore comes after the *Daily Telegraph* invented a similar row this morning,

accusing the Trust of dropping the name of the Christian festival from its annual Easter Egg hunt – even though it hadn't.

'We're just going to keep making up this kind of shite and hope some of it sticks,' said the paper's editor. 'Sure it's quare craic – even Theresa May waded into this one.'

We tried to contact the National Trust but they were all condemned to an eternity in hell.

21 ways to spot a Norn Iron person

One of the frustrations of being from Northern Ireland is being mistaken for someone English or Scottish when we're away somewhere foreign. Sure we speak roughly the same language, but we're far better looking, funnier and more attractive to the opposite sex. It's almost insulting that we need to make this guide to be honest … but just to avoid any further avoid confusion, here's how to spot a Norn Iron person.

1. They order a side of potatoes with lasagne.

2. When they meet another Norn Iron person they immediately ask them what school they went to.

3. When you ask them to do a message they come back with the weekly shop.

4. 'Lemonade' means any type of fizzy drink, including lemonade.

5. They'll always promise to 'give you a shout' at the end of a conversation.

6. They are unable to hang up the phone without saying bye bye about forty times.

7. Their mum phones them twice a day.

8. They phone their mum twice a day.

9. They think a mixed marriage is one between two straight, white people who were baptised in different churches.

10. Their granny still sends them a £20 note for their birthday, even if they are grown up and earning a clean fortune.

11. They like ten different types of bread on a fry and will pay over the odds to get them.

12. They say 'cheerio' to bus drivers.

13. They seem to be best friends with the driver of every taxi they get.

14. They exhibit cravings for a pint of Harp and a pastie bap every Friday.

15. When they go out for a pint of milk they end up in a riot.

16. They understand the correct response to 'What about ye?' is 'Aye, and what about ye?', and not your medical history over the past twenty-four hours.

17. They put the word 'wee' at the front of everything to make it seem like less hassle.

18. They'll start a conversation with a stranger at the bar, and end up being related to them.

19. They spend five minutes in the Chinese takeaway staring at the big menu on the wall before just asking for a half-and-half with curry sauce.

20. If there's a fire alarm/bomb scare/zombie apocalypse they'll be the ones arguing with the bouncers about why they should get to finish their pint.

21. They're usually a pale blue colour, then go red as soon as the sun shines three miles away.

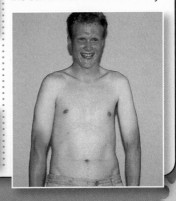

49

63 per cent of NI men currently shirtless, say police

As Ulster enjoys an almost unprecedented fifth day of sunshine, police have confirmed that two thirds of NI men are currently wearing nothing above the waist bar a watch they bought in Santa Ponsa one year.

'Our officer's body-cams utilise high-tech imaging software,' explained Bobby Peeler from the PSNI's Quare n Powerful Yokes Division. 'Aside from facial recognition of known criminals, we can also detect the outline of a bottle of Buckie stuffed down a pair of keks, spot someone skinning a joint, or lip-read phrases like "hide that de fuk, der's da peelers".

'But the latest update is the most ingenious,' he continued. 'We can detect the nipples of semi-naked humans from a

kilometre away. It's been going buck mental all week, so it has.'

A walk around the streets of Belfast confirmed the PSNI claims. 'I tuck one end of my rolled up T-shirt into my back pocket so it dangles around at my arse,' explained thirty-seven-year-old Bruce Street to us as he bought his second carry-out of the day at noon. 'I can just dander around showing off my leathery physique at local landmarks and places people go for lunch.'

Local office workers are delighted. 'As nice as the

Boots meal deal is, the highlight of my day is seeing oddly-shaped half-naked fellas hanging around City Hall,' explained thirty-two-year-old Ava Avenue. 'Add some bemused Spanish tourists who still look pure foundered in parka coats into the mix, and it's a real multicultural event. Belfast is getting dead cosmopolitan, so it is.'

Police have since confirmed that the couple responsible for yesterday's attack in Botanic Gardens were apprehended using the new technology. 'Facial recognition turned up nothing,' admitted Peeler, 'but your man's body piercing was in our criminal database.

'PSNI is probably the wrong acronym for us now really … we should be the NIPS.'

Belfast tourist hostage crisis continues

The whereabouts of dozens of tourists visiting Northern Ireland remains unknown at present after 'rival gangs' operating in Belfast city centre were seen forcing sightseers off the streets and into nearby vehicles earlier today.

The crisis began early this morning near Royal Avenue, after men in brightly-coloured jackets were seen approaching tourists and 'sweet talking' them onto nearby buses using glossy brochures and maps.

'I seen it all from my office window,' said Niamh Moore-Staples, a legal secretary from Stranmillis. 'I watched them bundle at least two dozen poor bastards on to a bus in broad daylight. I always

knew that the fella in the red coat was up to no good. He's a complete f**kin melter.'

Over two hundred tourists remained unaccounted for at lunchtime, although people matching their descriptions were spotted at random places throughout the city.

'We've had reports of them confusedly looking into the hole in the ground where we built thon boat that sank, asking locals why we named the airport after yer man who was class at playing football with a hangover, and gawking at a big f**k-off shed where they film all the bits

in *Game of Thrones* that would founder ye,' revealed Officer Jack Flackett from the PSNI.

'However we are pleased to report that all victims were eventually freed from their bus ordeal after a £10 ransom was paid.'

An arrest warrant was immediately issued for 'arseholes in red coats' – leading to the erroneous arrest of several Belfast traffic wardens. However, in a dramatic twist, police were forced to charge them with the crime anyway, after hundreds of angry drivers came forward to positively identify them as the culprits.

They were fined £90 – with a 50 per cent discount if paid within fourteen days.

Kendall Jenner to head up the Parades Commission

Centuries of tension over parading in NI may soon be a thing of the past after celebrity Kendall Jenner revealed she'll be handing out ice-cold cans of Pepsi over the Twelfth this year.

'I'm heading to Northern Ireland this summer,' she wrote on Twitter earlier today, 'to help bring about peace and stuff.'

Miss Jenner followed up her tweet shortly after having researched some Northern Irish slang particularly close to her heart. 'LOL. Someone just told me that NI people say 'Your ma's your da' all the time. #mykindaplace'

'We're absolutely delighted that Miss Jenner has agreed to help resolve parading disputes this year,' revealed Walter Cannon from the PSNI's Riots & Plastic Bullets Division. 'Usually we'd spend millions policing this shite, but she assures us she'll be able to sort the whole shebang out with a rake of cases of fizzy lemonade.'

However the Orange Order have dismissed this notion. 'Thon Pepsi tastes like dung. You can shove it up your arse!' said their head Cokesman, Willy Orr-Wontie.

His words have sparked fresh tensions between Northern Ireland's two opposing cola communities, who have been arguing for years about which is the most bitter, Pepsi or Coke.

Rory McIlroy to spend over £43 on lavish wedding

Star golf player Rory McIlroy is to blow an astonishing £43.60 on an extravagant wedding at a castle in County Mayo.

The superstar, who is marrying his fiancée, has told close pals that he intends to 'pull out all the stops' for the ceremony. *The Ulster Fry* understands that the pair spent £16 in the Connswater branch of Poundland alone, mainly on plastic plates, party balloons and a 'pre-owned' CD of 80s hits.

'He's really going for it,' said the megastar's close friend Jimmy Cricket. 'He's got a new tie and everything, although he's gonna try and get another run out of that suit he got for his mate's wedding four years ago. He's a bit chunkier now that he's crap at golf, but he's gonna get it let out by his ma.'

Gigantostar McIlroy is to splurge an estimated £2.99 of his budget on an astonishing fireworks display, as close personal friend Julian Simmons explains. 'He's got one of them indoor sets from Nutts Corner, the ones that curl out stuff that looks like dog poo. Some of the guests will even get a sparkler so they can try and write rude words in the air. Only about four of them will get one, though – he's not made of money.'

The Tyrannostarus Rex's wedding venue is a plush castle in County Mayo. 'Me and the lads built it on the beach yesterday,' said even closer personal friend who has known him for longer than the other two personal friends we interviewed, Gloria Hunniford. 'Its got four towers and flags made out of sticks.

'He should be used to flags, shouldn't he?' laughed Hunniford. 'They have them in golf, don't they? I think they do anyway.'

Rory McIlroy will be getting married at some point in the near future; we're not sure exactly when. BYOB.

Pope Francis and President Trump review Norn Iron's top tourist attractions

The Pope and President Trump hit it off so well during their meeting last week that they decided to go on holidays together – right here in Northern Ireland!

The powerful pair also agreed to review some of our best known visitor destinations, exclusively for *The Ulster Fry*. We think it's fair to say that their faces tell the story ...

1. Pickie Park, Bangor......................................

Trump: I enjoyed your Pickie Park bigly. I went on the swans and the disco ducks, then had a poke on the little golf course. Not the first time I've done that I'll tell yis. Definitely on my list of places *NOT* to nuke during my presidency.

Pope Francis: I had very much looked forward to zis place, but my cassock got caught in zee wheels of zee Pickie Puffer train and I was left wiz my erse hanging out. I weel not be back.

2. The Giant's Causeway

Trump: I loved your Giant's Covfefe. I haven't seen so many rocks since I was in the dressing room of *The Apprentice* with Gary Busey. Not so impressed with your Giant's Organ – it's nothing compared to mine. I mean, have you seen how big my hands are?

Pope Francis: Zis was sheet, just like your spelling, Meester President.

3. Titanic Belfast ....

Trump: Titanic – that's another word for bigly isn't it? Everyone all over the world knows about the *Titanic*. I like to think that my Presidency will be remembered in the same way as the *Titanic*.

Pope Francis: It's a sheep, it sank, what eez so good about it? You even had zee number that spelt No Pope backwards on it? Now you all go an as if putting 1,500 peeple on zee bottom of zee zee is as good as putting a man on zee moon. Yousuns are crezy.

4. The Craigavon roundabouts ....

Trump: Wow, just wow! I can't wait to get home and tell Melania all about these roundabouts. Maybe even bring her back some of your local wine – this place should be on everyone's Buckfast list.

Pope Francis: I mean, for Jaysus sake. You reely bring me here? I would rather turn Free P than come back to zis place.

5. The Derry Walls ....

Trump: These walls are amazing, truly, although I saw lots of DL registrations on the cars inside so the Mexicans are still getting through. Even so, I really enjoyed my time in Derry.

Pope Francis: Don't you mean Londonderry?

Prince Philip retires to spend more time at his caravan in Ballywalter

Prince Philip has decided to jack in travelling around the world with the Queen so that he can get more value out of his static caravan on the Ards Peninsula, *The Ulster Fry* can exclusively reveal.

'Me and Liz bought it a few years ago,' Mr Philip told us. 'We got it second hand on Gumtree from a fella in Lisburn – it was a real bargain at £7 grand, but he threw in the TV and a couple of gas cylinders so we wouldn't be starting from scratch.'

'It's thirty-five foot, like,' he continued. 'Sleeps four with room for the corgis, so the boy can come over with that new wife of his, but if any of the rest of the weans land in they'll need a tent. Now I've quit work we can come any time – just wing a few bags into the back of the Mégane and we're off.'

Since buying the mobile home the royal couple have spent many happy weekends in Sandyballs Caravan Park, where they've become firm friends with their neighbours.

'Sure they're quare craic,' said fellow camper Moira Station, from outside Moira. 'Phil's always up for a BBQ with a rake of beers, though herself is a bit of a wine connoisseur. Only

the finest stuff, mind – she has a footman pick out all the best numbers on the Bucky bottles.'

Park owner Kirk Cubbin told us that his regal guests have added a bit of glamour to his site, leading to many other members of the nobility renting plots.

'See that one over there? That's the Duke of Devonshire's, and the one beside it belongs to the Marquis of Salisbury. His cost near £12k, but it's got an awning and everything.'

However the newfound royal seal of approval is not without its pitfalls. 'Aye, they owe me £6 grand in pitch fees, the tight hurs. He keeps saying she'll pay, and she never carries any money.'

'Farmers' Tanning Salon' opens in County Tyrone

A County Tyrone businesswoman has opened what is thought to be the world's first tanning salon aimed at people working in the agricultural industry.

'It's a crowded market but I think I've spotted a gap,' says twenty-four-year-old Amanda Burns. 'Farmers here are famous for their unique tans – lower arms and the neck up only – but lots of them don't work outdoors. Instead they're stuck in mushroom tunnels, chicken sheds and barns full of pigs.'

'That got me to thinking, there could be money in this, so I've developed a tanning programme that recreates the look.'

Local agricultural workers have welcomed the news.

'It's a brilliant invention,' says Coalisland chicken breeder Roy Park. 'I was always embarrassed going to the beach with the other farmers: they'd have lovely red arms and faces and I'd be like a plucked Banty. Now I just pop in to Amanda's for a Farmatan™ and can get the same look.'

Users simply place their arms in elbow-length rubber gloves

filled with Amanda's patented 'Reddner Cream', before getting a unique facial spray. 'It's great,' says Roy, showing us the white line on his forehead left by the specially designed flat cap.

It's not only farmers who've been able to avail of the service. 'We offer a right arm and one side of the face service to taxi and van drivers,' says Amanda. 'Goes down well with anyone who spent the last fortnight in the pub.'

The Farmatan™ is only available at *The Burns Unit*, Amanda's salon in Dungannon. Prices begin at £14.99 an arm. Pensioner rates are unavailable; book early to avoid late booking fee.

The Ulster Fry

Bacon

The Ulster Fry

Norn Iron 'texting codes' the Police forgot to tell you about

The other day the PSNI released a handy guide for parents, supposedly warning them of the dangerous coded messages their teenage children may be using in text conversations.

We've been looking into it, and have discovered a rake of special local codes that the police forgot to mention. You may find them useful …

Family and Friends Chat

AYM – Aye Yer Ma

BFF – Big Fat Fecker

BYBL – Bout Ye Big Lad

GABAY – Giz A Buck At Ye

GYGY – G'Wan Ye Girl Ye

MAM – Me Auld Mucker

SIIL – So It Is Like

WAY – What About Ye?

Arguing

DUMD – Don't You Mean Derry?

FAA – F**k Away Aff

FART – Fancy A Riot Tonight?

IB8YBISIW – I'll Bate Your Ballix In, So I Will

L4AH- Looking for A Hiding

NIML – No I Mean Londonderry

YDSA – Yer Da Sells Avon

YMYD – Yer Ma's Yer Da

Wining and Dining

BYOB – Bring Your Own Buckfast

FLAPS – Face Like A Pastie Supper

GAMMY – Got Any MDMA On Ye?

GHB – Get Her Bucked

NOBONF – No Beans On Fry

Culchie Speak

CISSY – Clabbered in Shite, So Y'Are

HoSH – How's She Cuttin'

POT8O6 – Potato Sacks

QUAY – Quare Auld Yoke

TAROTITS – There's A Rake Of Them In The Shade

TC9T – The Craic's Ninety

WH8T – Wild Hate Today

Stormont Politics Specials

Thesuns are reserved for the secret communiqués of our MLAs.

BRB – Boiler Repayment Bonus

BTW – Blame Them Wans

COE – Claim On Expenses

CU@SB – See You at the Subsidised Bar

EXPATCOW – Ex-Prisoner Turned Community Worker

LMAO – Let Michelle & Arlene Organise

MLAs – Mostly Lazy Arseholes

MMIPS – Meet Me In The Pellet Shed

NOFMDFM – Any Empty Office

OMG – Offend More Gays

OSC – Occupied Six Counties

POV – Piss Off Voters

ROFL – Right, Off For Lunch!

TOS – The Other Surt

TSB – Those Shinner Bastards

TTMN – Tell The Media Nahin

DUP outraged as NI is overrun by leather-clad men riding up yer hole

There was anger amongst local homophobes today as thousands of men dressed in skin-tight leather outfits descended upon Portrush to shove motorised contraptions between their arse cheeks and chase each other around the town.

'We cannot stand idly by whilst our beautiful north coast is overrun by leather-clad men drinking beer and admiring each other's helmets!'

said DUP spokesman, Abraham Sammich. 'It's an absolute outrage … especially as they are also doing it on Sunday!'

'This festival of sodomy is an affront to the life of Jesus!' agreed Psalm Uel Jackson from the Mid-Ulster Church of Eternal Damnation. 'And to the memories of Peter, Paul, John, Matthew and all the other grown men he spent his days hanging around with!'

Intrigued, we travelled to Portrush to witness the sordid debauchery for ourselves.

'The town is filled with hairy men desperately trying to make a pass at each other,' revealed full-time eyewitness, Rosey Parker. 'Some of them must swing both ways too, cos they're trying it on the straights *and* the bends.'

Neighbour Ella Toupe agreed. 'It doesn't take a genius to figure out what is going on here. Grown men pitching tents in strangers' backyards … the smell of lubricant and burning rubber in the air – we're not stupid, ye know.'

A spokesman for *The Ulster Fry* has confirmed that they have now run out of homoerotic biker innuendo, but that readers are welcome to join in.

NHS Hackers 'unable to get past Northern Ireland doctors' receptionists'

The hackers behind the cyber attacks on UK hospitals gave up targeting the NHS in Northern Ireland after discovering they'd have to wait months to get access to computer systems.

'We originally planned to include your hospitals,' international cyber-terrorist Dell Tower explained to our security correspondent, 'but we were told we'd have to hack the computers of a GP first, then get a referral.

'We tried a local surgery but the receptionist emailed back saying that they'd no

appointments for a fortnight, and when we eventually managed to get past her the doctor said it was just a virus and to come back when we had something serious.'

The disappointed hackers were forced to give up on the NHS completely to focus on other targets instead, eventually managing to gain access to Northern Ireland's Education Authority. However, even then they didn't bother infecting the system.

'This is a ransomware attack, FFS, we're

supposed to make money out of it,' says Tower. 'When we saw your schools' bank balances we knew we were wasting our time.

'In fact, we deposited a couple of hundred quid so they can afford to buy pencils.'

8 great places to stop for a pish in Northern Ireland

Norn Iron has some of the world's best improvised pish stops, many of which (surprisingly) aren't listed on the Discover Northern Ireland website. We've compiled a list of the top places to stop for a slash whilst exploring our beautiful country.

1. Anywhere on the way to/from Kelly's, Portrush..............

No trip to Kelly's is complete without squatting behind a tree whilst cows watch you pee. Clubbers especially enjoy emptying their bladders on the Ballybogey Road, which provides natural cover and dense vegetation that doubles as 'organic loo roll'.

2. Jamesies Service Station, Glenshane Road ....

A safe-haven for motorists busting for a whizz between Derry and Belfast, Jamesies revolutionary 'split Portakabin' structure ensures men and women enjoy complete privacy – whilst flattened cardboard crisp boxes conveniently soak up pishy spray-back that might otherwise have ruined your shoes. (Also their sausage rolls are lovely.)

3. The back lane behind Laverys, Belfast

A classic late-night destination for many well-tubed locals, the lane behind this iconic Shaftsbury Square watering hole is one of the most popular places in the country to drop trou behind a bin. A definite must-pee!

4. Coach Inn Carpark, Banbridge....................................

If you've not taken a whizz at this famous Ulster hotspot then you don't know what you're missing. Actually to be fair no one who has actually pissed here remembers either … but still, don't miss out!

5. Up the Derry Walls...

Ancient, beautiful and steeped in centuries of heritage and history … none of this stuff matters a ballix when you are busting for a slash and doing a bar crawl in the Maiden City. Get up them stairs and find a dark corner.

6. Behind St Patrick's Hall, Dungannon

Whilst sadly having closed its doors to the public, St Patrick's Hall still serves a noble function after its rear wall was quietly converted into a urinal. This impromptu renovation job was carried out by Tyrone men using their own tools.

7. McDonalds, Coleraine..

There aren't many valid reasons to actually stop in Coleraine, but excruciating bladder pain is definitely one of them. This quick detour is perfect if you fancy Filet-O-Fish when you are filled-with-pish.

8. Applegreen...

Applegreen have revolutionised piss stops in NI with their fancy indoor bogs that have actually been cleaned; smiley-faced buttons that let you rate your pish; and the tantalising thrill of buying a Greggs pastie afterwards. They also sell moderately priced tea and coffee, ensuring that you'll probably need to stop at Jamesie's (see #2) for further piss taking.

Tensions rise in East Belfast after man erects two flags

There is growing concern among community representatives in East Belfast after a local man added a second flag to his home, and immediately declared himself '100 per cent more loyal' than his single-flagged neighbour.

The incident, which occurred in Aughrim Street, launched a run of tit-for-tat flag-related activities, which the PSNI fear may spiral out of control. Aughrim Street resident Walter Bunting takes up the story.

'It began this morning when Big Geordie at number 47 stuck an Ulster Flag up alongside his Union Jack,' he told us. 'It looks well, to be fair, one under each window at the front of his house, but he started hanging over the fence telling folk that he was twice as loyal as the rest of us.'

The move brought an immediate reaction from Wee Geordie at number 45, who erected three 20-foot flagpoles in his front garden, adding a Scotland flag to outdo his larger namesake.

'Wee Geordie's flags were fancy ones, too, with tassels round the edges,' says Bunting. 'He even got a bugle and played it as he hoisted them.'

The escalating tensions rose further when Average Geordie at number 44 got together with his neighbours, named locally as Dave and Davey, and they added fifty-two flag holders to the front of their properties.

'He's been on the internet and they've ordered the flags of all the Commonwealth countries, special delivery,' explains Bunting. 'And he's spelled out the words "No Surrender" across his house with them wee flags they have in the Navy.'

At time of going to press there is a heavy police presence in the area, although UN-sponsored talks have got under way in the hope of brokering a cease-flag.

Police promise crackdown on illegal culchie 'jives'

The PSNI has set up a special unit to deal with an upsurge in huge illegal dance events in rural areas across Northern Ireland, *The Ulster Fry* has learned.

The Division Against Non-legal Culchie Events (known as the DANCE squad) was established after twenty-three country music revellers were taken to hospital with first-degree foot blisters and dizziness following an illegal jive in Loughguile.

'There were an estimated three thousand culchies attending this event, each consuming their own body weight in tea and biscuits to reach a caffeine and sugar high required to hucklebuck all night,' stated senior DANCE officer Danielle Donnell.

'I have a lot of experience with these underground Marquee Jamborees. It's often very difficult to identify the offending partygoers, they sometimes bring up to eight double-collared shirts to each gig,' she added.

This task force follows a sting operation ten months ago, where 1,800 people were captured after being lured into a hole in a field in which the Marty Mone song 'Hit The Diff' was played repeatedly on a Sanyo CD Player. At the time, police spokesman Hugh O'Duncan said of the captives, 'All those arrested were barely able to speak. You couldn't tell if they were high, drunk or just from Strabane.'

Known as 'Jivers', the participants at these 'hoedown throwdowns' listen intently to country music radio, where DJs drop clues to the secret venues for the next gathering. Once the location is figured out, the message is soon relayed over CB radio to every tractor in the country.

A spokesman for the Jivers told us they were doing no harm to anyone, and that the events were just a way for 'folk to enjoy themselves in the summer.

'Not during the winter months mind you,' added the unnamed source, 'for you wouldn't be long getting frostbit.'

Tiger Woods 'on the rip' since McIlroy's stag do, say pals

Following his arrest yesterday, during which it appears US police dragged him backwards through a hedge, sources close to golfer Tiger Woods claim he's been 'on the lash' since Rory McIlroy's stag do in Magaluf.

'He'd literally just landed home,' revealed close pal, Wilson Staff. 'We told tour organisers he had a dodgy back to cover for him, but the truth is he fell in with a lock of boys from Glengormley on Rory's stag and went on a buck-mad bender. No one has seen him since!

'We eventually tracked him down by tracing his bank transactions,' he continued, 'which fluctuated between a Curley's off-licence, McDonalds at the Abbey Centre and a dodgy cash machine at the top of the Antrim Road.'

However Tiger's new best pal, Mackers Callaway from Rathcoole estate, reassured us that Woods is as committed as ever to his sport.

'He's been flat out practising. He hit at least a dozen new clubs in Magaluf and scored a load of birdies every time we went to a strip joint!

'In fact he must approaching his best form, cos I overheard him a few times saying he fancied smacking the hole on one.'

A spokesman for Mr Woods told us he'd be back in Northern Ireland soon, where he hoped to take up a new role in the sport. 'He quite fancies a job at the Pirate Golf in Dundonald,' said Alba T. Ross.

'Apparently it was the "yo ho ho" and the "bottle of rum" that swung it.'

'Our packets haven't shrunk, they're just further away,' claim Tayto

Amidst the news that over 2,500 UK products have gotten smaller in a phenomenon called 'shrinkflation', local crisp magnate Tayto has reassured customers that their packets haven't shrunk – they're just further away.

'Your arms are at least six inches longer now than when you were at school!' explained Tayto spokesman John Cocktail. 'So whilst our crisp packets might seem smaller now than in your heyday … they're actually just half a foot further away from your face!

'Plus look at the size of your hands, ya brute! They're like shovels … it's no wonder you finished the pack in two mouthfuls, ya big gulpin.'

Other local brands have also had to fend of criticism amid 'shrinkflation' pandemonium.

'Veda was always a futtery wee yoke!' stressed Irwin's spokesman Ted Baker. 'Our customers haven't been able to properly fit a slice of ham into it without folding it in half now for generations – so we resent being caught up in these scurrilous accusations.

'We downsized our product decades ago,' he added. 'Although to be honest no one has a clue why.'

Meanwhile, in a bizarre twist on the 'shrinkflation' saga, local Mexican restaurant Boojum have denied UPSIZING their famous burritos to hold *even more* food – after one man mentioned he was finding it harder to finish an entire meal.

'Our burritos are *exactly* the same size as they have always been,' explained Boojum spokesman, Aine Wrap.

'Yer man's just a lightweight,' she added.

10 insults that only make sense in Northern Ireland

Northern Irish people have given many things to the world – the sublime songwriting of Van Morrison, the silky skills of George Best, the sexy sofa-sitting of Eamonn Holmes. Alongside these giants of their chosen fields, we have also displayed an uncanny gift for insulting each other.

Some, like eejit, have become common currency on both sides of the Irish sea, but others remain impenetrable to non-natives. Here's ten to get you started.

1. Hallion...

A loud, ill-educated person, given to prolonged rants about subjects he or she knows little about.

Usage: Every time that hallion opens his bake I want to stick my boot in it.

2. Wab ....

Referring to the male member, it doubles as an insult. Also in use in Scotland where, like here, it describes most politicians.

Usage: The pair of wabs appeared outside the court dressed as Abu Hamza and, it seems, a kidnapped Jon Bon Jovi.

3. Tube
A good old-fashioned insult that describes someone who has a lot to say, but most of it is utter bollocks.

Usage: That sour-faced auld tube seems to get paid a wild lot for talking out of her hole.

4. Ganch
An irritating little tube who needs a good boot up the hole.

Usage: And the winner of the Brit Award for Biggest International Ganch is …

5. Dirtbird
A man who 'spreads his love' widely and indiscriminately.

Usage: Sure yer man's a right dirtbird. He'd ride the train to Bangor if it had a set of diddies.

6. Hoorbeg
The female equivalent of a dirtbird. A woman of easy virtue.

Usage: See yer one? Thon hoorbeg's seen more cocks than Moy Park.

7. Gack
A Derry wan. Someone who often comes out with a load of shite.

Usage: When did that wee gack get an American accent?

8. Gurn
Someone who complains a lot, usually with a sour auld face.

Usage: Tonight on *The Nolan Show* we discuss immigration, with a panel consisting of a slabber, a hallion, a gack and an auld gurn from North Antrim.

9. Spoon
Similar to a tube, and indeed a wab, but generally considered fairly harmless. See also moon cat and fruit loop.

Usage: I hereby declare this spoon elected MLA for West Tyrone.

10. Slabber
An individual who likes the sound of their own voice, even though the rest of us don't.

Usage: He's the biggest slabber in the country.

County Tyrone to get Ceefax 'by 2022' as part of DUP/Tory technology deal

The technology sector west of the Bann is set to get a major boost as part of the negotiations between the DUP and the Conservative Party in London, which will see £150 million paid out to provide ultra-fast broadband across NI.

'Or maybe that should be "Ulster-Fast",' admitted one of the DUP team.

'We're hoping to get full Teletext services for Tyrone within the next five years – at first it seemed the Tories were only going to pay for the east of the county but Arlene put her foot down and said, 'The

people of Castlederg deserve Ceefax,' and yer woman May soon crumbled.'

'This is great news hi,' said Dungannon business man Billy Clogher. 'A lock of years ago there was some chat about getting Superfast Fibre Optic Broadbrand in these parts, but it turned out it was just a delivery of Sunblest High Fibre

brown bread. It didn't improve our internet connectivity but at least it kept us regular.'

Traditionally viewed as one of the more neglected areas of NI when it comes to technology services, this is the second big boost to services in Tyrone in recent months.

In May the EE mobile network announced the installation of more than three thousand 'paper cups on string' communication hubs, allowing people up to two hundred metres apart to communicate incoherently with each other.

'Pretty much like we do when we're in the same room,' says Clogher.

Green Day cancelled by Parades Commission following mix-up

Tonight's Green Day gig in Belfast has been dramatically cancelled by the Parades Commission after being mistaken for a Republican rally, it has emerged.

'We read that thousands of people were gathering in Ormeau Park tonight for some big "Green Day" celebration,' explained Marge Banner from the NI Parades Commission. 'But when we couldn't find it on our system we freaked out and feared the Shinners had organised a huge protest over the Irish Language Act!

'However we realised we'd made a balls up when some boy called "Billy Joe" phoned up complaining about the cancellation,' she admitted. 'Thon's not the sort of name

you'd hear at the Ard Fheis like, is it?'

The PSNI were similarly caught off guard by the true nature of the event.

'We thought the exact same to be honest,' admitted PSNI officer Jack Flackett. 'When we Googled "Green Day" the top results were about being a "Minority", a "Working Class Hero" and a "Basket Case", which we were sure was stuff Gerry Adams says on Twitter all the time.'

To add further heartbreak for Green Day fans, a prominent Loyalist flute band is now playing in their place.

'We didn't think it was

fair for themmuns to have a "Green Day" and us not get an "Orange Day",' explained Billy Carson from the Ballybeen Purple Helmets, 'so we stuck in an application last week and it was accepted!'

However in a dramatic late turn of events, Green Day were granted permission to perform at the event as we went to press, subject to conditions.

'We've decided to allow it,' explained Banner. 'Provided they are okay with being re-routed, only play a single drum beat and don't play any of their big party tunes.'

5K to Couch:
The Ulster Fry guide
to getting out of shape

It's the Belfast marathon tomorrow, and lots of folk have been preparing for the fun runs and relays that go along with the big event itself. As a result everyone's Facebook timeline is full of normally lazy hallions angling after sponsorship for waddling a few miles, but that leaves a big question – how will they get back to their normal lardiness after all that hard training?

We've been talking to *Ulster Fry* 'fatness guru' Mr Procrastinator
and he's come up with a few pointers.

Eat a balanced diet

'Following the *Ulster Fry 5K to Couch*® diet plan is a key part of getting out of shape,' he says. 'A fried breakfast will set you up for the day, with a lunchtime top-up of sausage rolls to keep you ticking over. Teatime is chippy time, but don't forget those all important crisp-based snacks in between. Also, remember that you need at least five beers a day – wine also counts, but only the fortified monastic variety.'

Get a Fatbit™

The Fatbit™ works a bit like those Fitbit yokes, measuring key data such the number of steps you take, your heart rate and your sleep patterns – however the Fatbit™ issues warnings when

you're in danger of walking too far and wakes you up in the middle of the night to remind you to eat a pastie. Available soon from *The Ulster Fry* shap at a bargain price of £299.99, excluding postage, packing and instructions.

Build up your lack of stamina

'Sitting on your hole is vital,' Mr Procrastinator explains, 'but it's important to take it slowly or you'll risk injury. Start off sitting in an armchair for short periods, then move on to lying on the couch. Your body will naturally tell you when you reach your hole-sitting peak by making you stay in bed eating Haribo while watching *Homes Under the Hammer*.'

Download a load of TV box sets

Even the laziest among us can get bored during periods of intensive training, so Mr Procrastinator advises a solid library of classic television. '*Game of Thrones* is my favourite,' he told us. 'It has diddies in it and everything.'

Finally: never give up!

Sooner or later everyone hits the wall and accidentally gets some motivation to do healthy activities. 'Don't yield to temptation,' says our man. 'That piece of fruit could be the first step on a slippery slope towards exercise. Some fitness gurus say *pain is temporary but glory is forever*, but I say *pain* is the French word for bread so go and make a crisp sandwich.'

5K TO COUCH
AN ULSTER FRY DIET PLAN

ULSTER FRYS
START EACH DAY WITH A DELICIOUS FRIED BREAKFAST

SAUSAGE ROLLS
EAT 3 STANDARD SIZED SAUSAGE ROLLS EACH DAY - OR 6-9 MINI ONES 'N' NOT AVAILABLE

PASTIE BAPS
EAT CHIPPY FOOD AT LEAST ONCE EACH DAY

CRISP SARNIES
DEPOSIT ONE WHOLE PACK OF CRISPS BETWEEN TWO 'ROUNDS OF WHITE BREAD 2-3 TIMES A DAY.

BEER
DRINK SEVERAL PINTS OF LAGER BEFORE BED.

23%
14%
26%
22%
15%

10 reasons why getting to bed drunk is a whole handlin'

Everyone loves a good night out on the rip, except Jim Allister obviously, but while we're out spilling pints over ourselves we all forget that it has to end at some point and sleep will be required.

Sadly, knocking back all those drinks has made us forget that we've turned a routine ritual into a complex manoeuvre that can result in injury, divorce or – in the worst cases – sleeping under the dog on the sofa.

Fortunately a team of craic scientists at the Getting Blocked Department of Sixmilecross Bible College have been looking into the problem and have come up with this little guide so we all know what to expect. Forewarned is forearmed.

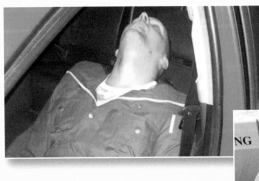

1. Getting out of the taxi is virtually impossible.

2. Once inside, that 'quick slice of toast' and 'one wee bottle of beer' before bed turns into a full fry-up and half a bottle of whiskey.

3. You suddenly have an overwhelming desire to learn about the history of 1970s disco music on BBC4, until 3 a.m.

4. Eventually you've had enough of Boney M and decide to go to bed, but if there's more than one light switch in the hall, you try them all before going upstairs in the dark and leaving the outside light on.

5. You think there's an extra step when you get to the top of the stairs and fall into the dirty-washing basket.

6. Your shoelaces become more complicated, particularly as you've attempted to remove your jeans over the top of your shoes.

7. You spend twenty minutes trying to charge your phone using a cable from a Nokia 3310 you had in 1998.

The Troublemaker I have something misguided and angry to say about this current event. I'm posting it here because I know it will start a giant debate, and I am super bored.
Yesterday at 11:16pm · Comment · Like

The Bait-Taker You're wrong. You're the most wrong person ever. I had an uncontrollable urge to tell you that even though I can feel myself getting pulled into something we'll both regret.
Yesterday at 11:29pm

The Troublemaker Wrong? Are you kidding me!? I plagiarized that word-for-word from something my talking head of choice said on his or her cable news show last night!
16 hours ago

The Chime-In I agree with Troublemaker because he

8. When you check your phone 'one last time' someone has posted something you disagree with so you end up in a two-hour argument about the effects of Brexit on horses.

9. Your plan to drink a pint of water before bed means you have to get up for a slash twenty minutes after finally getting to sleep.

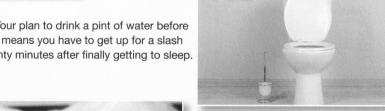

10. It's only then that you realise you're in the wrong bed, in the wrong house and have to apologise to the couple next door.

The Ulster Fry

12 things every Northern Irish person does on a 'farin halliday'

Farin hallidays. Everyone loves them, but we all end up
doing the same old shite. Recognise any of this?

Airport beers

The best beers ever. It doesn't matter what time
it is, you're on your hallidays so start as you
mean to go on.

Forget stuff/get overcharged for replacement

'43 euro for sun cream?'

'Sí señor. Now, do you wanna wee beg wi lat?'

Get burnt on the first day, then spend the rest of the holiday trying to stay in the shade

It's in our genes, and we forgot the sun cream and refused
to pay 43 euro for it.

Make best friends with folk from home on the first night then spend the rest of the week trying to avoid them because it turns out they're melters

Although, to be fair, half the time they're thinking the same thing about you.

Get a hangover off local shite

Then bring a bottle of it home to keep under your sink for the next ten years.

Buy immense quantities of holiday sweets and crisps

Lie on the balcony horsing strange Wotsit-like things intae ye, washed down with dumpy cans of some beer you can't pronounce.

Go looking for a proper fry

But end up getting a full English because thesuns don't understand real food.

Regret going to an Irish bar

'Aye, we'll just call in for one' usually descends into twenty-three pints of Guinness and a sudden desire to sing 'The Fields of Athenry'. Then next morning you have to hurriedly delete the video evidence and hope the lads in the Lodge won't see it.

Go on a shit excursion to look at dolphins but get pissed and forget about dolphins

Sure you can see dolphins any day of the year, but on this beer is included in the price.

Get mistaken for being Scottish

Okay the accents are similar, but they're not that similar, ye ballbag.

Try to work out if you could afford to move there

'Aye sure, we could open one of them Irish bars, there's not enough of them here.'

Finally, start thinking about having to go back to work about three days into the holiday …

69

Ancient Norn Iron tapestry revealed by historians

Following news that *Game of Thrones* now has its own Bayeux-style tapestry in the Ulster Museum, prominent historians have revealed that they already had a very similar artefact in storage.

Dating from the twelfth century, The Buck-you Tapestry tells the story of life in Northern Ireland in medieval times. As these scenes show, nothing much has changed.

Controversial Bonfires

Shit kicking off in Lurgan

YE LARNE FERRY

Folk bringing carry-outs to Old Firm games

YE ELEVENTH NIGHT

LURGAN

Folk getting writ aff

THEY DIDST ALL GET BLOCKED

KFC

PRIMARK

YE PRI MARK

Dodgy voting at elections

LO, I VOTETH IN THIS BOX, AND I VOTETH IN THIS BOX.

Feck all happening at Stormont

Bargain hunting

The weather was usually crap, and 'weather prophets' were treated like gods

YE TALKS AT STORMONT

BEHOLD YE WEATHER FORECAST

AYE YER MA

NO, YER MA

YER DAS SELL AVON

And there were always quality insults

American golfer Graeme McDowell's ancestry traced to County Antrim

Patriotic local golf fans got an unexpected new hero at this week's Irish Open, after historians discovered that US golfer Graeme McDowell's ancestors are actually from the County Antrim town of Portrush.

'Well, gee whiz, that's fantastic,' McDowell told local press. 'My grandpappy used to tell us stories bout the ol' country when we were little 'uns, but darn tootin' I was too busy shootin' eagles to pay much attention to the old critter.

'But slap my thigh I've sure been enjoying this lil' course y'all built here,' he continued. 'It reminds me of the one I played on as a boy!'

Northern Irish sports fans were overjoyed with the news, immediately claiming the Yankee sportsman as one of their own.

'His grandfather and mine went to the same school,' revealed Pat Stewart from Portstewart. 'They used to play golf together too, until after one excursion up to City of Derry Golf Club, Graeme's granda suddenly started calling him "mucker" and adding "hi" to the end of all his sentences. He couldn't listen to him after that.'

However some greeted the news with cynicism. 'He's only been here ten minutes and he's already got a bit of a Norn Iron twang to his accent! Typical bloody Irish-American!' commented Irish golf journalist, Enda Rough.

McDowell has not taken the allegations lightly though. 'Y'all be tripping, fool,' he shot back on Twitter this morning. 'I came here to do my talking on that there golf course, so I did … and dognabbit imma madder than a rattlesnake I didn't make the cut today. Ya know whadda mean, like?

'Ya ballbeg,' he added.

Reportedly seething with jealously at his countryman's newfound popularity in NI, fellow American Rory McIlroy has started looking into his own genealogy.

Local football fans torn between love for both Linfield and Celtic

Thousands of football fans across Northern Ireland find themselves in a severe quandary today as their two favourite sides prepare to meet in a Champions League qualifying match.

'There's a real crossover in the fan base of both clubs,' we were told by Scottish football pundit Jocky Fullerton. 'It's true you get the odd Linfield fan who supports Rangers, and maybe the occasional Celtic supporter who prefers Cliftonville, but generally it's hands across the North Channel for these two clubs.

'Even that famous Irish song, "The Sash", that's about a guy from Belfast going over to Glasgow to watch Celtic, I think.'

Many fans we spoke to still have no idea who they'll support tonight.

'I grew up steeped in the history of Celtic and Linfield,' revealed Lisburn Road man Andy Row. 'My da was always telling me stories about the Lisbon Lions and all that, so it'll be a real struggle to take sides. Lots of the lads I spoke to on the Twelfth are feeling the same way.'

Falls Road native Conway Mills is similarly torn. 'I've supported the Blues since I was a kid,' he told us, 'I'll never forget the first time I walked into Windsor Park, it was like a religious experience for me, except with Buckfast instead of Communion wine.

'To be honest, it's just as well Celtic didn't take up their allocation of tickets; there'd be no point as half the Celtic fans in Belfast are season-ticket holders at Windsor anyway.'

The first-ever meeting of the two clubs is at five o'clock tonight, with an early kick-off arranged to allow Linfield fans from Dublin to catch the last train home.

9 amazing facts about Derry

It has the more names than anywhere else in the universe

Derry, Londonderry, Legenderry, Doire, The Maiden City, Stroke City, The Walled City and more. Even people who live there don't know what to call it without starting an argument. A whopping 92 per cent of divorces in the city start over disagreements about where they live.

Every sentence ends with 'hi', hi

Derry wans are incapable of ending a sentence without saying 'hi'. The late Bruce Forsythe famously banned Derry people as contestants on *Play Your Cards Right* as they couldn't go low without going hi as well. However he did allow Derry women on to *Strictly* as they like to tango themselves.

Everyone lives three doors away from their ma

Derry's property market is boosted by a complex and never-ending system of 'house swaps', which ensures everyone lives within a hundred metres of their ma. It is estimated Derry mas are currently owed £4.7 trillion by their grown-up offspring.

They love strangely-named baked goods

Gravy rings, German buns, turnovers and snowballs. None of these things make sense to the outside world, but in Derry they are part of a 'nutritious' breakfast – typically eaten at 7 a.m. ... out of a greasy white paper bag ... with a hangover ... whilst driving a van somewhere ... to buy sausage rolls.

It's illegal to serve food without a side of tobacco onions

Over 90 per cent of the onions in NI to are sent to Derry for 'tobaccoisation' – a process in which local women peel and chop onions whilst chain-smoking Lambert & Butlers and gossiping – before going to get fried somewhere. The onions meanwhile are sent off to be cooked in really hot oil.

75 per cent of men are personal trainers

Almost all men in Derry work in the fitness industry and claim to have invented dieting and exercise. Of the rest, 15 per cent work as photographers taking photos of them in their underpants, whilst the remaining 10 per cent have them both blocked on Facebook.

82 per cent of women are make-up artists

Most Derry women are employed by each other to do one another's make-up in a complex house of cards that leading economists warn will topple when they realise they can simply do it themselves.

People go to the pub at midnight

Derry socialites don't go near the pub until at least 11.30 p.m. – preferring instead to meet in someone's living room, where they drink cans of Harp and shout over the top of each other until someone runs out of booze and phones a taxi.

Derry's biggest news source is its Facebook 'Buy It Sell It' page

Originally used for selling shite that people had laying around the house, Derry's 'Buy It Sell It' page has evolved into a community noticeboard for spreading rumours, outing cheating husbands, finding out which Chinese does the best curry sauce and creeping on random strangers. It's rumoured to be where Seamus met his last girlfriend.

Twelfth crisis: No pallets left to actually deliver pallets, warns City Council

There was widespread panic across Belfast this morning after the city council admitted they'd run out of actual pallets to stack bonfire pallets on to, in order to transport them across the city.

'Literally all the pallets in Northern Ireland are now earmarked for burning,' admitted council spokesperson Enda Brownbin. 'We had a rake set aside in the back parking lot for shifting the rest, but some hallions broke in last night and nyucked em!

'The thieving hurs phoned us this morning to come collect 'em until they need 'em again,' he continued. 'They're out in the yard now with the rest.'

The news comes as a blow to Belfast City Council, whose staff have been fastidiously storing pallets at a secret facility whilst simultaneously ignoring that someone wearing grey trackie bottoms and Nike Air Max had previously beaked school to steal them.

It is also a huge source of concern for residents living near bonfire areas, who now face the daunting prospect that they may not get to board up their windows with plywood or watch drunken teenagers having awkward sex by firelight behind a busted sofa.

'It's a worrying development,' admitted Paul Etstack from the PSNI's Bonfire Support Unit. 'There is simply no way to get them loaded on to trucks now. We've had to send the forklift drivers home!'

With the crisis deepening by the hour, Loyalists have set up a GoFundMe page to finance the purchase of new emergency bonfire materials in time for the Twelfth.

Donations are welcomed through PayPallet.

Incredible discoveries as *The Antiques Roadshow* comes to Stormont

Producers of *The Antiques Roadshow*, due to arrive in the Stormont estate on Saturday, have requested an extra day of filming time after their researchers discovered ninety unusual antiques in the basement of Parliament Buildings.

The hit BBC show, presented by newsreader Fiona Bruce, appraises antiques brought in by local people and other artefacts found in the building in which the show is being filmed.

Mrs Anne Teek, a researcher for the *Roadshow* told us, 'We were over at the Stormont estate this week for a pre-production meeting when we decided to visit the canteen,

located in the basement of Parliament Buildings.

'Upon opening the doors, we were astonished to find approximately ninety dust-covered antiques just sitting around on chairs in the canteen. We immediately called in the help of an expert who told us they may be what is known locally as an *MLA*.

'Apparently, whilst they may not have any intrinsic or monetary value, each MLA does have its own individualities, traits and uniqueness. Some of them are known to date as far back as 1690 whilst others may be from the post-1916 era. We have requested some additional time and resources to research these relics in a bit more detail.'

A spokesman for the Stormont Estate said: 'These antiques have been lying in the basement doing nothing since the Assembly Election back in March 2017. They're just gathering dust and, if I'm honest, the place is starting to stink up a bit. Hopefully they'll be shipped out soon enough as they're now starting to cost us a fortune in storage.'

The
Ulster
Fry

Soda

'Gosh, the DUP seem horrible,' gasp people who voted for poverty, corruption and NHS cuts

Tory supporters across the UK are 'extremely concerned' it has emerged, after Googling the Democratic Unionist Party and discovering they are even more hateful than the people they voted for.

'I'm absolutely disgusted,' revealed thirty-one-year-old Tory fan Branston Pickle. 'I mean, blocking a woman's right to have an abortion is terrible. It's only fair you allow children to be actually born before you stop giving a shit about their welfare!

'I can't believe they banned gay blood donations!' revealed Rita Daly-Mailey. 'It's good manners in England to bury your homophobia deep down and pretend to be offended when "gay" is used as a derogatory term. How have they managed to get elected by just being themselves?!'

It also seems that terrorist links are suddenly a concern for Tory voters.

'I was shocked to find out the DUP were endorsed by paramilitaries last week!' revealed Zach Bencher. 'I mean okay, so we crucified Corbyn for his tenuous link to republicans whilst overlooking the fact that Theresa May is selling weapons to the Bank of ISIS ... but at least she made us a few quid to help keep the country safe from them! Right?'

However not everyone was so gloomy about the coalition.

'I think the DUP are an excellent fit,' revealed Conservative voter, Oz Deritty. 'I was reading about that Renewable Heating scandal, and they showed a real aptitude for allegedly taking the tax contributions of working-class people and investing it into their friends and benefactors instead. I think they'll fit right in!'

Despite this, many Tory voters remain unconvinced by their new DUP allies. 'I took a heart attack when I seen that photo of Sammy Wilson!' revealed cardiac arrest victim, Ann H. Mess.

'But it's okay,' she assured us. 'The ambulance should be here any day now!'

American tourists devastated to find 'Sandy Row' is not a beach

An American family holidaying in Belfast have been left shocked and confused to find that the famed 'Sandy Row' they'd been hearing so much about is not in fact a beach, but a historically loyalist residential thoroughfare.

'We feel totally deceived,' said Hank Thunder, the family's patriarch. 'People kept telling me that this was where all the "Orangemen" go and we assumed it was some sweet tanning spot. I came here to get my tan on.'

Mr Thunder's claims were lent credibility by the fact that he'd been strolling around the neighbourhood for several hours clutching a lilo with a pair of incredibly disappointed, sun-cream-lacquered children in tow.

'It's infuriating,' he continued. 'Things are so difficult in the US right now. We just needed to get a relaxing break from the horribly caustic and divisive political atmosphere, so we came to Northern Ireland.'

It is understood that this is not the first disappointment the Thunder family have suffered on their trip so far. Holywood locals reported seeing a distraught-looking American family walking through the area angrily complaining at the lack of celebrities to be seen, shouting 'What is this nonsense? Not even Liam Neeson? They can't even afford a second "l" for their signs!'

In a related story, members of a French family who booked three weeks in a caravan site in Larne have also expressed their disappointment, but not for any comedy mix-up reasons.

'Eet was just sheet,' they told us.

Apprentice Boys finally set to become Fully Qualified Tradesmen

The Apprentice Boys are set for a dramatic re-brand, *The Ulster Fry* has learned, after it emerged that *all* of their members are now fully qualified tradesmen.

'We finally graduated this summer!' revealed former Apprentice Boy Lorcan Gates after today's march around the walled city. 'We managed to arse about playing pool and smoking fags in the students' union of the North West Regional College for about two hundred years or so – and the craic was great, don't get me wrong – but eventually we had to knuckle down and get our diplomas.'

The news has been warmly welcomed by their exhausted parents. 'Thank ****!' exclaimed relieved mother, Sasha Violet. 'He's been hanging around here eating us out of house and home for centuries now, leaving clothes at his arse and expecting me to pick up after him. Well he can fend for himself now he's got a job. We're moving to Portrush!'

The Apprentice Boys organisation is now set for a complete restructure as a result of the mass graduation.

'We're going to have to start paying everyone a proper wage now,' moaned Newbuildings man Mitchell Burne. 'Plus there'll be no more sending the young wans for a long stand, tartan paint or left-handed

screwdrivers,' he sighed. 'It's the end of an era really, but we're hoping to pick up some bigger contracts now everyone is finally legit.'

However better wages and fewer practical jokes aren't the only changes for former Apprentice Boys.'We got the absolute bestest news EVER this morning!' revealed Newly Qualified Boy Geordie Walker. 'Turns out we get to join the Union as well!'

Government proposes new pallet wall along border

The UK government is considering the construction of a huge wall of pallets along the Northern Ireland border as part of its Brexit strategy, *The Ulster Fry* has learned.

As our slightly poor artist's impression shows, the structure will be up to thirty pallets high in places, with small gaps to allow people to look at sheep that live on the other side.

'We decided to take a different angle on the whole "customs"

border thing,' said a senior Tory. 'We know that you lot have a custom of collecting pallets in the summer, so we thought this wall might blend into the landscape. Plus you can burn them once a year.'

The pallet wall is one of a number of ideas proposed by the government today, which they claim will maintain a seamless border on the island. These include:

• Free movement obtained through the electronic tagging of everyone on the island. This will ensure that Theresa May knows where everyone is at all times, and can tell them to go home.

• A 'small trader customs exemption' for goods transported using a new donkey-based courier service that will carry things across the border in baskets like you see in old photos.

• The legalisation of smuggling, 'so we don't have to worry about any of that auld shite'.

• Hiding under the bed and pretending nothing is happening.

The Irish government is also said to be considering a 'cultural customs' border, with a plan to build a wall formed entirely from massive GAA sportsbags and people doing *Riverdance*.

No one from the Stormont Executive was available for comment.

10 (other) Catholic things that Protestants should never say

So it seems the Orange Order has advised Protestants to avoid saying 'Rest in peace' on the grounds that it's a Catholic thing and not Biblical.

That got us to thinking what other things Catholics come out with that should be banned for Prods. Here's 10 we came up with.

1. 'Jesus, Mary and Joseph'
A traditional Catholic expression of surprise, often followed by "Would ye look at the arse on that?".

2. 'Anyone up for a big game of Gaelic football after Mass?'
Protestants should never say this. They should say 'Anyone up for a big old game of proper football *the day before* that new pastor preaches in the gospel hall?'

3. 'The crisps in Dublin are far nicer than the ones at home'
Mr Free State Tayto is an immoral charlatan sent by Satan to draw children to his evil ways.

4. 'North of Ireland'
Protestants must only say Northern Ireland, which is different from the North of Ireland. They can also say Ulster, which is different from Northern Ireland but is the same as the North of Ireland. They definitely can't say Occupied Six Counties.

5. 'Who fancies a pint this Sunday afternoon while we all watch some sort of sport?'
This is wrong on so many levels.

6. 'Derry'
Goes without saying so don't say it, at least not in front of themuns.

7. 'I'm just heading out for a Sunday walk without my hat'
Going out for a walk on a Sunday is fine, but ladies must wear hats AT ALL TIMES.

8. 'Teacakes'
Teacakes and other such individually baked confectioneries are fundamentally unbiblical. Protestants should only eat traybakes, as these are in Matthew, Ch. 5, v. 6, when our Lord fed five thousand people with a rake of caramel squares.

9. 'Holy Mary Mother of God, would you ever turn that music down, ye wee shite?'
This was once a common Catholic phrase used when speaking to teenage children. Increasingly it has been replaced with 'Holy Mary and all the angels, do you ever take those f**king earphones out?'

10. 'Haitch from Steps'
It's Aitch, although to be honest we asked him once on Twitter and he never replied one way or the other.

10 Protestant things no Catholic should ever say

Opposite is a list of Catholic phrases that no self-respecting Protestant would ever use. Here's the 'other-ways-round' version.

1. The Mainland
When referring to England, Scotland and Wales. The only Catholics who refer to the Mainland live on Rathlin, or on a boat.

2. 'Fiddlesticks, I've forgotten my hat'
Proper Protestants are notoriously crap at swearing, instead making up words like 'Jumping Jehosaphat' and 'Sugarpuffs' instead. This is bollocks – or balderdash, if you're a Protestant.

3. 'Our wee country'
You mean Occupied Six Counties surely.

4. 'Roman Catholic'
Only Protestants say this, as they claim Catholic means all the churches. Catholics must insist that they are the only Catholics, as they know that the correct word for everyone else is a heretic.

5. 'I don't like that new vicar, I think I'll start going to the Presbyterians instead'
Protestants are never done changing churches when they fall out with a clergyman or decide they don't like some new rule. Catholics don't have that option, even if the new priest goes on and on about how much better his county is at hurling.

6. The Queen
You can only refer to 'the Queen of England', you can't imply she's queen of here.

7. 'Fancy going for a wee drive and a poke this Sunday, darling?'
Protestants love going for Sunday drives, usually in search of ice cream. However, according to rules set out in the Second Vatican Council, Catholics can only spend Sundays in the pub or at GAA matches – after Mass, obviously.

8. 'There's nothing I like better than a big sausage supper after work on a Friday'
Fish suppers only on a Friday. To do otherwise is to risk eternal damnation and/or funny looks in the street.

9. 'Where's the Twelfth this year?'
It's at your caravan in Donegal, unless you live near a contentious route in which case you need to stay home to be offended.

10. 'Could you pick me up a *News Letter*? I want to see who's dead.'
Catholics can only buy the *Irish News* so anyone dead will be in there. The only exception is on a Saturday if you want to check the price of fat yos in the *Farming Life* section.

Exam board to offer GCSE in understanding GCSE results

The Council for the Curriculum, Examination and Assessment (CCEA) has been forced to introduce a new qualification that will help parents and pupils understand the GCSE process.

They announced the plan this morning, after thousands of bewildered families received results letters.

'Apparently I've got 196 in Biology Unit 1A Higher Intermediate Geography,' we were told by fifteen-year-old Luke Stumped. 'Seems this is a D, but it's only worth 15.673 per cent of my total mark, which I get after I do Unit 234 next May.'

'I haven't a baldy what any of this means,' was the reaction of confused mother Nora Clue. 'My Jack seems to have got an A* in Foundation Heart Surgery (Module 1.2C), even though he didn't sit the exam.'

A spokesman for CCEA claimed that the results were easy to understand.

'Look, you've got a column here which shows the subject, one for the module, then the mark, then the grade,' said the Council's Head of Bollocks, Barra Graph. 'For example, if you want to get your final grade for Chemistry, all you have to do is add together the marks for Units 1, 3, 5 and 2, then allocate a weighting to each module, then multiply by 6 and divide by 12.

'Then you just have to go to our website where you'll find a series of cryptic challenges and a treasure hunt. If you complete all these tasks, you'll be rewarded with an envelope containing the same figures that you started with.'

The new GCSE in GCSE Studies will begin next September. Students will be expected to complete 132 modules by November, when they'll begin coursework that will contribute 83 per cent towards one third of their final mark.

New airline 'exclusively for drunk people' to operate out of Belfast

Amid news that an increase in arrests for drunken behaviour by passengers may lead to restrictions on the sale of alcohol on flights, a Belfast-based airline has launched a service aimed exclusively at plastered travellers.

QueasyJet will operate flights to several popular holiday destinations, including the Canary and Balearic Islands, Greece and Corfu.

'Getting snattered at the airport is an important part of every holiday,' slurred Harvey Wallbanger, the entrepreneur behind the venture. 'Why else do airlines ask you to turn up two hours before your flight leaves? It's to give you time to get writ aff!'

'Just because a few people take things too far by groping staff and fighting each other that shouldn't spoil it for the rest of us, but I can understand how being surrounded by a load of people boking their rings might be unpleasant for sober passengers.

'We'll get around that by making sure that *everyone* on my airline is rubbered by the time they board, and that includes the cabin crew and pilots.'

Local inebriated travellers have welcomed the news. 'Fuppin' brilliant sur,' said a man we met in the bar at Belfast International Airport, who had just ordered pints of gin with vodka chasers for his wife and three children.

'Yousuns are my best friends, so yis are, yis bastards,' he concluded, before punching us and vomiting into his hand luggage.

QueasyJet's first flight left Belfast this afternoon, four hours late as several passengers had to be rounded up with cattle prods. It later ditched off the coast of Portugal after the pilot mistook 'a big slap of watter' for Lanzarote Airport.

11 words that mean something different in Norn Iron

It's a well-known fact that Northern Irish people have the sexiest accent in the world – you only have to look at the likes of Liam Neeson, Gloria Hunniford and Frostbit Boy. We always have the right word for every situaitchun, even if it means something different to the rest of the world.

1. Air
Normal Meaning: A mixture of nitrogen, oxygen and other gases that forms the earth's atmosphere.
Norn Iron Meaning: A period of sixty minutes.
Usage: 'Ah'll see ye in halfin air.'

2. Bangor
Normal Meaning: A slightly crap seaside town in Wales.
Norn Iron Meaning: A slightly crap seaside town in Northern Ireland.
Usage: 'Are ye goin' te Bangor fur yer haldees again this year?'

3. Battle
Normal Meaning: A military engagement.
Norn Iron Meaning: A glass or plastic receptacle for liquids.
Usage: 'Give us a battle a Harp an a packet a cheese an onion.'

4. Clatter
Normal Meaning: A loud noise, a racket.
Norn Iron Meaning: A number of items, somewhere between a rake and a wile lock.
Usage: 'Go an git us a clatter of thon wee futtery yokes from the shade.'

5. Flak
Normal Meaning: Anti-aircraft fire, sustained abuse or criticism.
Norn Iron Meaning: A group of sheep.
Usage: 'Wild shepherds watched thur flaks by night.'

6. Hearst
Normal meaning: William Randolph Hearst, a US newspaper mogul 1863–1951.
Norn Iron Meaning: A mid-Ulster term for a long, black funeral car.
Usage: 'Are ye doin' a lift from the Hearst at the funral?'

7. Pitchers
Normal Meaning: Large jugs.
Norn Iron Meaning: Photographs or paintings. Also the cinema.
Usage: 'Is that new Trainspattin' fillum on in the pitchers?'

8. Raisin
Normal Meaning: A partially dried grape.
Norn Iron Meaning: An excuse or explanation for an activity, often lacking.
Usage: 'She bait me fur no raisin.'

9. Shack
Normal Meaning: A dilapidated structure.
Norn Iron Meaning: A sudden scare or surprise, also electrocution.
Usage: 'It'll be a quare shack if themuns bait us on Saturdee.'

10. Straight
Normal Meaning: Without a bend, angle, or curve.
Norn Iron Meaning: A row of houses.
Usage: 'It's all kickin' aff on are straight the night.'

11. Stirs
Normal Meaning: The act of mixing a liquid in a circular motion.
Norn Iron Meaning: Steps used for moving between the floors of a building.
Usage: 'Get you up them stirs before ye feel the backa ma hand.'

The Ulster Fry

10 things you never knew about Northern Ireland: a guide for English folk

With all the political shenanigans at Westminster, loads of English people are suddenly interested in the goings-on in Northern Ireland. We've put together this handy primer to help them understand this complex place.

1. Northern Ireland has a population of 18 million, divided into Protestants, Catholics and Others. Protestants want Northern Ireland to be part of Scotland and Catholics want a united Ireland. No one cares what the Others think.

2. It is part of a small island off the English Coast that was discovered by St Patrick in 1423. Patrick was a British man who is now the patron saint of Ireland. Protestants who like Britain can't stand him, whereas Catholics who don't really like Britain think he's the best thing since sliced bread. (Look, just go with it.)

3. The capital is Belfast, where they made the movie *Titanic*. The two other largest cities are Derry and Londonderry.

4. The two biggest political parties are the DUP and Sinn Féin. The DUP are now in charge of running England and pretty soon Sinn Féin could be in a coalition in the Irish Republic, but neither party is in government in Northern Ireland. This is called power sharing.

5. The main language is ballix, spoken by over 84 per cent of the population. The remaining 16 per cent speak Tyrone, a dialect so complex even fluent Tyronians can't understand each other.

6. The national pastimes are drinking, arguing, and arguing while drinking.

7. Our most famous tourist attraction is the Gigantic Causeway – a huge stone structure formed in 4000 BC during the Great Flood.

8. The most famous Northern Irish actor ever is Eamonn Holmes, who has appeared in movies like *Taken*, *Taken 2* and *Fifty Shades of Grey*.

9. The singer Van Morrison is from Northern Ireland. After leaving The Doors in the 1960s he invented the Ford Transit.

10. Our greatest ever sportsperson is George Best, who played for Man Utd in the '50s before taking up snooker and changing his name to Alex Higgins. Famously good-looking, it is estimated that Best slept with 76 per cent of women in England.

There, that should give everyone a bit of background. Now you can get back to arguing about the DUP.

Rioting in Belfast amid fears of sausage roll ban

There has been sporadic rioting in parts of Belfast today after it emerged that an English primary school has banned sausage rolls from its pupils' lunchboxes.

It is understood that people took to the streets after learning that Shirley Manor Primary in Bradford had introduced the ban, fearful that it would soon spread to the rest of the country.

Many areas saw panic buying of the savoury delicacies this morning, but this was followed by looting after bakeries began to run out. Violence was inevitable, and several branches of Greggs have been forced to close in what the PSNI have described as 'the worst baked goods-related disturbances since the Gay Cake riots of 2015'.

'It's a slippery slope,' said angry protestor Phil O'Pastry shortly after throwing a stale iced finger at a police Land Rover. 'It starts with sausage rolls, then it'll be the jambons. Before you know it they'll be banning Paris buns. And we all know what that will lead to – anarchy.'

The trouble has since spread to other parts of the country.

In the North-West the protest has crossed the traditional sectarian divide, with people united against the savoury tyranny. Even the famous Free Derry corner has been amended to 'You are now eating in Free Derry/Londonderry.'

Meanwhile, disgruntled lorry drivers are blockading Jamesies Services at the Glenshane Pass.

'We won't move till we get assurances from the government that we'll be able to stock up on lardy snacks as we see fit,' said truckers representative Leyland Daft.

'They may take our pies, but they will never take our freeedoooom,' he concluded, whilst running at police lines wearing a kilt.

Ryanair chief to receive Honorary Boot up the Hole Award

Ryanair Chief Executive Michael O'Leary is the bookie's favourite for the 'People's Choice' prize at the annual Boot up the Hole Awards ceremony, organised by *The Ulster Fry* website.

Mr O'Leary has been nominated for the gong following his decision to cancel his airline's flights from Belfast to London until next March, despite having already sold lots of them.

In a statement Mr O'Leary apologised profusely for the cancellations, but said that it would ensure that 99 per cent of his airline's passengers would be unaffected.

'Except you f**kers,' he should have added. 'We don't give two shites about you f**kers.

'We'll get this sorted as soon as possible,' a Ryanair spokesman probably said. 'Anyone who has lost their flight just needs to log on to our website and pay a small cancellation fee, then we can process their refund, less tax.'

'Then, by way of compensation, we'll give all affected passengers a special voucher which will allow them to book a Ryanair flight which will then be cancelled at a later date.'

The prestigious 'Holey' awards have been awarded by *The Ulster Fry* on an annual basis since 2017, with recipients receiving a 'good boot up the hole' for their lack of service to the wider community.

As well as Ryanair, this year's nominees include Stormont MLAs; whoever invented the roadworks on the Newtownards Road; and anyone over the age of thirty who uses a skateboard.

Commuter rescued after three days stranded in Belfast traffic

A Comber man has been airlifted to safety after spending several days stuck in the perpetual traffic jam that is usually called the Newtownards Road.

It is understood that forty-two-year-old Billy Hackamore left his home around 4 a.m. on Thursday morning 'hoping to beat the traffic' but became stranded at the roadworks at the Knock traffic lights.

'I thought I'd given myself plenty of time to get into the city centre,' he told *The Ulster Fry*, 'but it turns out that if I wanted to make it in for nine I should have left in October 1623.'

Mr Hackamore's ordeal continued into the evening, at which point he decided to stay put in the hope that he might make it to his office in time for work on Friday morning.

'Sadly I was wrong, and when I wasn't home on Saturday the missus finally phoned the police who arranged for me to be lifted by a Coastguard helicopter.'

The Department for Infrastructure has confirmed that commuters can expect 'long delays' on their journeys to work.

'We're proud of our record in ensuring that East Belfast remains in a permanent state of gridlock,' said DfI spokeswoman Leanona Brush. 'In fact we added a few random extra roadworks on the Albertbridge Road just to delay you a bit longer if you escape the main ones.'

We asked Ms Brush how long drivers can expect to endure these delays.

'At least until Hell freezes over,' she told us, 'which, if they're lucky, might be early January as, if it does, we probably won't bother our holes gritting it.'

PSNI to enforce controversial new 'Sunday Driving Curfew'

There were jubilant scenes across Northern Ireland today, after the PSNI unveiled a revolutionary new 'Sunday Driving Curfew', which will force people who don't actually know how to drive properly to do it before noon each Sabbath day.

'Now that we're not always knocking seven shades of shite out of each other,' explained top traffic cop Jerry Datsun, 'policing in NI has finally turned its attentions to the really important issues facing *both* sides of the community here.

'Such as cracking down on people who drive like clampits.'

Under the new scheme it will be illegal to cause a tailback after noon on a Sunday, whilst anyone found driving *under* the speed limit after midday will be issued with a fixed-penalty notice – and a good boot up the hole. There have also been other sweeping changes.

'To cut down on administration, certain models of cars are simply banned from the road after the curfew!' continued Datsun. 'These include Nissan Micras, Fiat Unos, Toyota's Aygo, Hydundai i10s – plus any other vehicle also powered by the motor of a second-hand washing machine.

'If you own one of these shitewagons our advice is to either get out early, or just stay at home!' he stressed.

However the move has also angered many, who say that it could spell the end for the long-held NI tradition of 'going for a poke' on Sunday.

'I've been driving around in second gear looking for an ice cream for decades!' revealed Bangor pensioner, Gina Genelli.

'I've yet to find the place though,' she added. 'Do you have a map I could borrow?'

'Huge hole' at centre of Great Pyramid 'may be Portadown', say Archaeologists

Top archaeologists working in Egypt believe that the 'huge void' they have discovered in the centre of Khufu's Pyramid may be the County Armagh town of Portadown.

The experts believe that the mysterious hole may finally confirm their theory that the entire pyramid complex was built to contain the greater Craigavon area.

'We have long known that the ancient Egyptians feared the evil forces that lie within Craigavon,' says chief archaeologist Howard Carson. 'We have already found relics that prove that they had

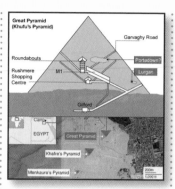

enclosed Lurgan within the Great Pyramid – this would seem to be the final piece of evidence that we need.'

As this diagram which we found on the BBC website

shows, many major Craigavon landmarks are housed within the structure, including the M1 and Rushmere Shopping Centre.

Portadown woman Sandra Gee said that she was surprised to find that she was living in the middle of an ancient Egyptian structure.

'Who'd have thunk it? I mean, lots of people round here walk sideways and have heads like cats, but I'd never have believed this was possible,' she told us, using hieroglyphics.

'I can't wait to tell my mummy.'

Complex World Cup draw 'designed to keep you lot apart', confirms FIFA

The world football authorities have admitted that their massively complicated second-place play-off formula was designed to ensure that the two teams in Ireland wouldn't meet at any point.

'It was okay when Northern Ireland was vaguely shit,' says Hans Ball, the FIFA vice-president responsible for corruption. 'We knew all we had to do was rig the draw to make sure you weren't in the same group, but then they started beating people again, and things got more difficult.

'We had a bit of a scare at Euro 2016, so we added the "seeding rule" to the play-offs as we thought that the chances of either of your countries having one of the top four second-place teams

in Europe were pretty slim. If you're both in the bottom half of that "mini-league", then we're sorted.'

The plan almost fell apart when Northern Ireland accidentally reached twentieth place in the World Rankings.

'We were literally shitting our keks,' says Ball. 'All they had to do was beat Germany and Norway and it'd all go diddies up. Fortunately, we were able to bribe both those teams to win and you were safely in the bottom half.'

Phase two now kicks into action, as FIFA intends to rig the play-off draw to ensure that both Irish sides get ridiculously difficult opponents.

'The Russian authorities have paid us handsomely,' explains Ball. 'Their police don't fancy having both your teams in the same group next year, and apparently there isn't enough beer in Moscow to cope with the fans.'

The British and Irish governments have welcomed the news.

'The peace process is flimsy enough,' said a spokesman. 'A late winner by Kyle Lafferty or James McClean would set us back decades.'

8 things Northern Ireland does better than Germany

You might have noticed that there's a massive match at Windsor Park this evening, with Germany taking on Northern Ireland. It'll be a big test for a squad of relative unknowns drawn from some of Europe's less glamorous teams, as they face some of the world's greatest players in a crucial qualifier. Hopefully it won't be completely embarrassing and, with tight defending and a bit of luck, Germany won't lose too heavily.

Anyway, just to get everyone warmed up, here's a rake of other things we're better at than Germany.

Food

Fans who've made the journey from Germany to Belfast are in for a real gourmet treat. They'll be demanding '*Das pastie baps*', '*Der filled sodaskermench*' and '*packets uff das yellow Tayto*' from Angela Merkel as soon as they get home.

Bands

All that oompah shite pales into insignificance when you see the wide variety of marching bands on display here. Flutes, accordions, flutes, pipes, more flutes. And do Germans have Lambeg drums? None that we're aware of anyway.

Walls

The Berlin Wall was erected in 1961 and lasted till 1989, a mere twenty-eight years. We've been successfully dividing ourselves for over forty years now, and have even made our walls into a tourist attraction.

Cars

Porsche, Mercedes, Audi, BMW – Germany is famous for producing high-powered cars that drive right up your hole on the road between Ballynahinch and Newcastle. But can any of them time travel?

Roads

Germany has thousands of miles of *Autobahns*, whereas our motorways will only get you as far as Dungannon or Randalstown. Despite this, our roads are better because at least we drive on the right side of them, which is the left, right?

Words

German is a completely mental language compared to Norn Ironish. For example, *Schadenfreude* is the German word for taking pleasure in someone else's misfortune, whereas when someone screws up we just shout 'yeoooooooo'. They don't even have a word for scundered.

Sexy football

You'd be forgiven for thinking that the four-times World Champions have had the better players over the years, but they didn't have the Best.

Hospitals prepare for epidemic of 'Underwhelmed Tourist Syndrome'

Local hospitals are gearing up for a flood of severely disheartened travellers after the *Lonely Planet* guide named Northern Ireland as the world's top destination for 2018.

Doctors fear an outbreak of a rare disease called Underwhelmed Tourist Syndrome, which can flare up when the brain releases the chemicals that govern the feelings of disappointment and anger at the same time.

'These chemicals collide in the victim's frontal lobe, rendering them completely speechless and unable to smile for photographs,' says top physician Dr Ben Dover.

'We first saw it among visitors to Carrickfergus in 1985, but it most commonly strikes when tourists first set eyes on the Giant's Causeway.

'They suddenly realise it's nothing like the misty, mystical photos they've seen on the internet – and that they're standing in the rain staring at a windswept pile of oddly shaped rocks when they could have gone somewhere warm instead.'

Hospital staff are concerned that UTS sufferers could be a huge burden on the already overstretched Health Service.

'If people follow the advice of this guide we could be inundated,' says Dr Hugh Wontfeelathing from the Ulster Hospital. 'This *Lonely Planet* shar also have Belfast on the list of "must-see destinations".

'Sure we don't even have that big wheel at City Hall any more – our biggest attractions are a ship that sank, a large bap and a river that sometimes doesn't smell like shite.

'That said, if they're disappointed after queuing for our tourist sites, they're in for an even bigger shock when they see the size of our hospital waiting lists.'

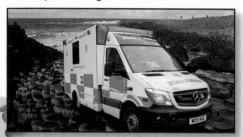

Coalisland at centre of offshore tax haven scandal

Top celebrities have been exploiting legal loopholes to hide millions of pounds in secret offshore bank accounts based in the County Tyrone town of Coalisland, a huge leak of financial documents has revealed.

Dubbed the 'Peat Bog Papers', the documents name many of the world's richest people, including the Queen, Bono, Gary Barlow, Ma from *Give My Head Peace* and that guy who does the voiceover on the adverts for Brennans Bread. All are alleged to have taken advantage of Coalisland's lax financial rules to squirrel away millions of pounds.

The Ulster Fry, along with some other global media outlets, has gained access to the documents. Our investigation team has been investigating, and has managed to find some astonishing facts.

• The Queen has over £500 in Coalisland Credit Union. It is understood that she hopes to double this by next April, then get a loan for a car.

• Roman Abramovich has hidden £4.3 million in Baler Twine Holdings, a shadowy investment fund that owns 21 per cent of Dungannon Swifts FC. Officials at the English FA are concerned that this may be a conflict of interest with his ownership of Chelsea, as the two sides could meet in the Champions League.

• Bono and Ma from *Give My Head Peace* have both sold items on Coalisland Buy and Sell, with the U2 front man scooping over £12 for a load of old wine bottles that he'd covered in glitter. None of this was declared to the taxman.

Local businessman Pete Land-Park was astounded when we told him that celebrities were using Coalisland to pay less tax.

'Fecking amateurs,' he commented, 'I haven't paid tax at all since 1964.'

Prince Harry reveals lavish Northern Ireland wedding plans

Officials at Buckingham Palace have stunned the world of royalty by announcing that Prince Harry will break with convention and marry his fiancée Meghan Markle in a gospel hall outside Banbridge.

The Prince has already visited the district, and is understood to be weighing up his options for the reception.

'Harry's undecided between The Coach and The Belmont,' said seasoned royal watcher Wanda Butler. 'Chances are there'll be a load of culchies in The Belmont, but he reckons he'll be able to have a carry-out in the car park which will save him a few quid.'

Bride-to-be Meghan Markle, daughter of German Chancellor Angela Merkel, is believed to have her heart set on a honeymoon in the County Down fishing village of Annalong.

'She loves the place,' says Butler. 'Her ma bought a caravan there when she was over for that G8 summit a few years ago, so she's practically grown up there. It's a bit isolated for most celebrity types, but sure you just have to hop on the bus and you can be partying in Kilkeel or Newcastle in no time.'

It also looks like the wedding won't be the last we see of the royal couple in Northern Ireland, as the ginger prince and his bride hope to set up home here after the big day.

'Harry's got a job lined up in Almac,' explains our expert, 'and they're on the list for a house in Craigavon.'

We texted Prince Harry to ask him about his plans but he didn't reply – he mustn't have topped up his phone.

Northern Ireland style 'deli' opens in Paris

A top French chef has opened a fashionable new Parisian restaurant that only serves delicacies traditionally found in Northern Irish petrol stations.

Forty-three-year-old Marco Peure Shite told us that he came up with idea while holidaying here last summer.

'Oui,' he said (instead of yes). 'I often stopped at your garages, and noticed that they all have a type of deli which is unique to your part of the world.

'In Paris, a delicatessen will sell les fancy cheeses, les olives, les gourmet meats … but in Irlande du Nord they have an incredible range of lard-based products, wrapped in pastry or stuck in un bap.'

Situated on the Champs Elysées, as it's the only French street we know, Le Filling Station has been fully booked since it opened, with Parisians flocking to enjoy sausage rolls, bacon baps and filled sodas.

'C'est magnifique,' restaurant critic Henrietta Jambon told us. 'I had le "lorry driver special" – a chicken curry and chips topped with a sausage, delightfully presented in une yellow styrofoam box.

'For dessert I may have un Pear Picking Porky, a gravy ring or perhaps one of your traditional pokes – maybe a mixture of all three,' she revealed. 'Although I'm told that you should never have a poke *in* your gravy ring, unless you're feeling particularly exotic.'

If successful in this venture, Marco intends to import more Northern Irish cultural delights to France.

'We have plans to hold "Le Festival de l'Orange" next July,' he revealed. 'Hopefully Monsieur Mayor will give us a grant to buy a rake of pallets.'

PSNI investigate multi-million pound Pick 'n' Mix heist at Continental Market

Police have launched a major investigation after thieves made off with sweets valued at over £35 million from the Belfast Continental Market Pick 'n' Mix stall.

The officers believe that a 'highly sophisticated group of criminals' carried out the audacious heist, targeting only high-end items.

'The Continental Market is famous throughout the world for its ridiculously expensive confectionery,' said Chief Superintendent Bertie Basset, from the PSNI's Half-Serious Crime Squad. 'Anyone who's accidentally bought a quarter pound of vanilla fudge from the vendors will know that their purchase can end up costing several thousand pounds.

'These criminal masterminds seem to have been planning this heist for months,' he continued. 'They've dug a tunnel from the toilets of Burger King, under Donegall Place and the City Hall lawns, before finally emerging just below the arse of Queen Victoria's statue.'

Once inside the market the thieves ignored other ridiculously expensive items, such as glass cases full of overpriced knitwear and safes packed with carved wooden shite, making straight for the Pick 'n' Mix.

It is believed they then filled holdalls with millions of pounds worth of macaroons, Turkish Delight and unusually-shaped handmade truffles that no one would ever dream of buying at other times of the year.

The PSNI has urged everyone to be vigilant.

'We urge everyone to be vigilant,' said Basset. 'If anyone approaches you offering sweets that you wouldn't normally eat but might fancy "because it's Christmas", please get in touch with your nearest police station.'

The Ulster Fry

Potato Bread

New mural on Sandy Row as Jackie Chan becomes loyalist icon

Martial arts star Jackie Chan is the surprising new hero of unionism after single-handedly taking on the 'Authentic IRA' in Netflix's film *The Foreigner*.

The movie sees sixty-three-year-old Chan star as Quan, a businessman who embarks on a mission of revenge after losing his daughter in an IRA attack. As a result, Mr Chan is now so popular in loyalist circles that his image has replaced King Billy on a gable end in Sandy Row.

The hero worship hasn't ended there, with an East Belfast flute band now named in the star's honour.

'He's a quare lad,' said Carson Wiliamson, the bass drummer of Ballymacarret Red Chan Defenders. 'We're even thinking of changing the words of 'The Sash' so it becomes "The Black Belt Wee Jackie Wore".'

Mr Chan is understood to be bewildered by his newfound status, though he is considering moving here. 'Jackie's not sure about the whole loyalist thing,' his agent told us, 'but he has his eye on a caravan in Millisle and he might apply for a job as a community worker if there's a grant in it.'

In a related story, dissident group Óglaigh na hÉireann have finally got round to calling a ceasefire amid rumours that Chuck Norris is thinking of coming out of retirement to film *Delta Force 4* in South Armagh.

However a senior republican source denied that the veteran star would ever side with the British. 'Tiocfaidh ár Norris is one of ours,' he told us.

Trump to visit Ards Shopping Centre instead of London Embassy

Donald Trump has sensationally scrapped plans to fly to London for the opening of the US Embassy, preferring to take a much-needed break on the Ards peninsula.

Speaking exclusively to *The Ulster Fry*, the controversial President revealed that he'd been planning the visit for months, and that there was 'no way some new embassy was going to interfere with me getting round Woolco'.

'I'll probably park Air Force One at your Newtownards Airport then get a taxi over to the mall,' he told our US correspondent Randy Wankelfecker III.

'There's some great stores there now, they've got a Poundland *and* a B&M Bargains, so I'll be able to pick up a souvenir or two for Ivanka and whatever my son is called.'

Mr Trump also plans to take in a few of the Peninsula's more glamorous sights during his trip.

'I'm hoping to catch the bus to Comber,' he revealed. 'I've heard from some very reliable friends, good friends, that they do great potatoes there, and it's only two letters away from the word combover.

'Then maybe I'll head down to the great port of Ballywalter for a poke. I can absolutely guarantee you that I'll have the biggest poke in the whole peninsula. With sprinkles.'

However the president's visit isn't just for pleasure as he also plans to conduct some high-level business.

'I've plans to invest in one of your biggest golf courses,' he told us. 'By the time I've finished, Donaghadee Putting Green will be hosting the British Open.'

Mr Trump also used the interview to deny calling several African countries 'shitholes'.

'I was referring to Craigavon,' he explained.

Northern Ireland 'will be one giant pothole by 2022' warn experts

Northern Ireland is well on the way to becoming the world's largest pothole, a major international conference was told today.

Addressing the World Holeiologist Society, Professor Gar MacAdam told his fellow experts that a lack of roads investment 'combined with shite weather' mean that the entire province could disappear within five years.

'Not many people realise it, but Lough Neagh started

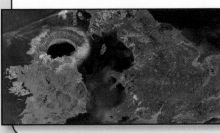

out as a minor pothole on an ancient road from Antrim to Cookstown,' he explained. 'Sadly no one in the Bronze Age could be arsed patching it up, and it gradually expanded until it became the massive watery hole we all know today.'

Recent research has revealed that our entire transport infrastructure is under threat.

'We estimate that 84 per cent of the rural road network here is made up of holes,' says the professor. 'The remaining 16 per cent consists of slivers of tarmac held together with cow dung, with the odd cat's eye sticking out of it at a weird angle.'

The claim comes on the same day that the

Department for Infrastructure admitted spending nearly half a million pounds on compensating motorists whose cars had been damaged by the poor road surfaces.

'We've at least two reports of vehicles vanishing completely,' revealed a DfI spokesman. 'In one case a lorryload of chickens drove into a pothole near Broughshane, only re-appearing six weeks later in a South African diamond mine.'

Professor MacAdam had one final word of warning.

'If Lough Neagh keeps expanding at its present rate, we can expect to see towns like Antrim, Crumlin and Ardboe disappear off the map completely,' he concluded. 'So it's not all bad, I suppose.'

Breakthrough as local woman discovers how to put toilet seat down

Scientists across the globe are hailing a 'major breakthrough in human development' after a County Antrim housewife became the first-ever woman to work out how to put a toilet seat down.

Forty-two-year-old Wanda Pish made the discovery when she went to the bathroom on Thursday morning, only to find that her husband had once again left the seat in the upright position.

'I was about to give out to him, but then something stopped me,' she revealed. 'I suddenly realised that there was some kind of hinged device at the back of the seat, and saw that I

might be able to lower it myself if I was careful. It took about twenty minutes mind you, but hopefully next time I'll have it in place before I wet myself.'

'Ever since the invention of the toilet, it has been assumed that only men have the necessary skills to put the seat down,' says Professor Lou Brush from the Thomas Crapper Institute for the Advancement of Toilets.

'In fact, there are cave paintings in France that depict ancient women yelling at men for not putting the stones back round the hole in the ground, so Wanda's achievement could be a game changer in gender relations.'

The discovery could have benefits for the global economy, Professor Brush explained.

'It must be remembered that a man putting the seat up for use, then back down, requires two separate movements, whereas a woman putting the seat down requires only one. Literally seconds of time could be saved, leading to a major boost in productivity in workplaces where there are mixed facilities.'

In a related story, the man who wrote this story is no longer able to sit down in any capacity, having been given a severe boot up the hole.

The Ulster Fry Guide to ... County Tyrone

In the latest instalment of our in-depth guides to all things Northern Ireland, we tell you eight fascinating facts you never knew about County Tyrone.

1. Tyrone is the only Northern Irish county visible from space.

That's right, it's the biggest of the six counties. In fact it is so big that you could fit Australia, the USA *and* Wales inside its borders and still have room for some sheep, as this photomap proves.

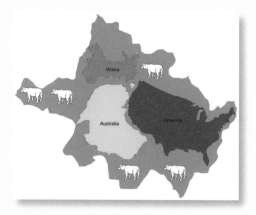

2. Despite this, it has the lowest number of people compared to the other five counties.

Tyrone is the only known county in Northern Ireland that has more sheep than people, with an incredible 3.4 million sheep but only 14 actual people. This is as a result of something called emigration, which led to loads of sheep moving there in the 1820s.

3. Tyrone is home to one of the world's most famous crystal glass manufacturers.

In 1843 Dungannon man Billy Crystal discovered that most couples wanted ornate glassware as a wedding present from elderly relatives, and opened a factory producing it in his shed. That factory is still running 150 years later, and is called Waterford Crystal.

4. Some of Northern Ireland's most famous people are from Tyrone.

Philomena Begley, Hugo Duncan, Malachi Cush, Jedward and that girl who got into bother in Peru are all from Tyrone. Why is Tyrone so good at producing famous people? No one knows.

5. Tyrone is the best county in Ulster at Gaelic Football.

They're so good at it that experts believe that even a team of Protestants from the county could kick the arse of the other teams, if they could be bothered.

6. One Tyrone town is still at war with Germany.

When the great powers sat down to sign the Treaty of Versailles in 1919, they forgot to invite Plumbridge. As a result the First World War is still raging in the heart of the Sperrins, with locals regularly digging trenches to repel the Hun.

7. The national currency of Tyrone is turf.

No one in Tyrone leaves home without at least six sods of turf in their pockets. They use it to barter for luxury goods like beer, clothes and more turf. This means that Plumbridge people are the richest in the county as they have loads of turf from the trenches they dig for fighting the Germans.

8. The county has its own language, called Tyronistanian.

The last person to speak any recognised international language in Tyrone died in 1934. Since then, everyone in Tyrone has communicated by saying 'Hi bai' and waving at each other from cars.

Stephen Nolan caught hiring voice actors to make bigoted phone calls

Protestants and Catholics actually 'get along grand' claims an undercover investigator, who says community tensions in NI are perpetuated by a team of voice actors who phone into radio stations to rant bigotedly.

'We've discovered that a group of actors have been redialling *The Nolan Show* and putting on Cullybackey, Glengormley and Castlederg accents – in a bid to keep the show ratings up,' said Alastair Dineen of Ofcom. 'It's been going on for years – and there is evidence that the BBC and local media are in on it.'

We spoke to one of the actors. 'I used to phone the show about three or four times a day,' he told us. 'It was a real cushy number. Just phone in, be angry, and totally disagree with the other person. My favourite character was an irate Belfast taxi man called Big Jim.

'I didn't even know if I was going to be a Prod or a Taig till I got through,' he admitted. 'I'd just disagree with the other person's viewpoint, recite a load of oul sectarian rhetoric, get everyone shouting at the radio, and then wait for the cheque to land!'

However many of the voice actors recently quit because they got tired of arguing about the same thing over and over again.

'Aye, we got bored saying the same oul shite to each other,' he told us. 'We really just wanted to get along with each other in the end up. We're all good pals now and meet up like normal people.'

Due to the actor shortages, the remaining *Nolan* callers must now assume *both* sides in current radio debates, rapidly changing their accent in an effort to contradict themselves.

This revelation has angered both Sinn Féin and the DUP, who were quick to issue a joint statement that contradicting themselves was *their* job – shortly before retracting it and apologising.

Craigavon man who wore coat indoors loses benefits

A County Armagh man has been stripped of all benefit entitlements after ignoring repeated warnings about wearing his coat indoors.

It is understood that government inspectors spotted forty-three-year-old James Barbour wearing a Parka jacket whilst watching television at 11 a.m. this morning.

'We immediately issued him with a benefits warning letter,'

says David Trench from the Department for Coats (DfC). 'These explain that "you have the right to wear a coat indoors, but if you do so you are unlikely to feel the benefit of that garment when you go outside, should you chose to do so".'

Mr Barbour now admits that he ignored this advice.

'As soon as I stepped outside I was clean foundered,' he told us.

Inspector Trench says that these types of scams are becoming a major problem for the authorities.

'We're even seeing people attempting to claim coat-related benefits while in work: a clear breach of the regulations,' he explained.

As a result, the DfC has teamed up with YMRC (Yer Mammy's Rituals and Customs) to set up a special hotline that allows members of the public to report neighbours they spot breaking traditional rules that their ma used to set when they were wee.

'If you see anyone not eating their crusts, not going to the toilet before going on a long drive, or crying before they're given something to cry about, you can call us on 0800 123 321,' says Inspector Trench.

'On the other hand, if you break your leg while doing it, don't come running to me.'

8 ALMOST INTERESTING FACTS ABOUT COUNTY DOWN

The Ulster Fry guide to ... County Down

1. Newsreader Moira Stuart is so popular in County Down that they named the town of Moira after her. They had planned on calling it Stuartstown but her fans in County Tyrone got in first. A state of war has existed between Down and Tyrone ever since.

2. Named after a local hotel, Slieve Donard is the highest mountain in Northern Ireland. At an incredible 850 metres high, it is the 65,432nd highest mountain in the world. Only three people have managed to climb it but no one knows who they are.

3. County Down contains three of Northern Ireland's poshest towns – Hillsborough, Holywood and Bangor. Every year they hold a special 'Posh Towns' Challenge' to see which is most up its own hole, with events including Drinking Prosecco while Riding a Horse, Name Dropping and Lobster Wrestling.

4. Much of *Game of Thrones* is filmed in the Mourne Mountains, but it's not the only time that County Down has provided a big-budget location. The seedy Mos Eisley Cantina in *Star Wars* was filmed in the Coach Inn, Banbridge, and the entire *Lord of the Rings* trilogy was made in Rathfriland, with the famous water tower used as the Dark Tower of Sauron.

5. The favourite hobby of County Down people is 'going for a burn up the town', a strange ritual which involves driving round a town centre to see who's about while listening to either Nathan Carter or obscure dance anthems from the 90s.

6. Down is the only county in Northern Ireland with *nearly* three cities – as it has parts of Belfast, parts of Lisburn and all of Newry (apart from the wee bit in Armagh). Both Lisburn and Newry were made into cities in 2002 as part of the Queen's Golden Jubilee celebrations when she got pissed and Prince Philip bet her she wouldn't do it.

7. County Down man Harry Ferguson is often credited with inventing the tractor. In doing so he also invented the rural traffic jam by ensuring that all country roads are permanently blocked by farmers hauling huge steel tubes full of shite or pieces of machinery that can barely fit between the hedges.

8. On old maps of Ireland the Ards peninsula was called the Ards *peni*sula, because it looks like a willy. When the government changed it to peninsula in the 1960s the people of Ballywalter rioted for six weeks in protest.

DUP demands 'Sash Wednesday' as part of Stormont talks deal

Talks at Stormont have taken another twist after the DUP demanded that Protestants should also be able to paint their foreheads with a cultural symbol tomorrow, in what one party source has nicknamed 'Sash Wednesday'.

'If Catholics are allowed to come to work looking like dicks, then we demand the same,' revealed East Antrim MLA Willy Samson. 'For too long now we've stood idly by whilst Catholics get to arrive late for work – or get cushy breaks to go see a priest. It's nat on, so it's nat.'

It's understood that hundreds of Ulster's Orange Halls will be put to full ceremonial use for the occasion, so that both sides of the community can begin Lent by queuing up to have their foreheads smeared with a badly drawn symbol that instantly identifies their religion.

Surprisingly Sinn Féin are fully on board with the proposal.

'Usually, if you want to know what surt someone is, you have to ask complicated questions about what school they went to, or maybe challenge them to a game of "Office Countdown" to hear if they say haitch or aitch,' explained their North Belfast representative Kerry Gelly. 'Now, for one day a year you can tell just by lukking at 'em.

'Which I always could do anyway,' she boasted, 'but it takes years of practice to get this bitter.'

Belfast pub 'The Spaniard' to be deported after Brexit

Northern Irish drinkers were left furious after reports emerged that one of Belfast's most treasured places to not swing a cat is being sent home because it's a foreigner.

'Si, señor, they have told us to pack up our sheet and get out,' confirmed The Spaniard's head barman Miguel Whataboutye. 'We eez no longer an EU pub, so we're nat.

'Es is mucho whole handlin,' he added.

The news comes just days after sickening racist graffiti appeared on the exterior wall of the immigrant pub, including 'White rum is better than dark rum' and 'Take your Dark & Stormys back to where they came from'. The vandalism is thought to be handiwork of far-right drinking group, Britain Thirst.

'We only drink in *loyal* establishments such as The Duke Of York, The King's Head and The Crown,' revealed a spokesman. 'Them foreign-sounding pubs can f**k right off!'

However The Spaniard won't be the only local establishment affected by 'Beer-exit'.

'The Europa Hotel is getting kicked out on its hole too,' confirmed leave campaigner Morgan Spice. 'And The Washington Bar will have to close its doors unless it can negotiate a new trade deal with President Trump.

'The crafty hurs have an ace up their sleeve, though,' he revealed. 'They've sneakily offered to sell him The Northern Whig.'

Late speculation that Mr Trump is in bed with the Russians was not helped by shocking photos of him getting debriefed in the Kremlin.

NI Protestants to get their own XXX 'Durty website'

A County Antrim businessman has launched an X-rated website aimed squarely at Northern Irish Protestants.

Ballymena entrepreneur Bertie Oldman told *The Ulster Fry* that he believes that he's spotted a gap in the market.

'The worldwide interwab is full of wild durty wabsites that cater to all manner of tastes, but there's nothing for upstanding members of the Ulster Protestant community.

'I spent months looking at these sites, then herself came home from work early one day, and I suppose you could say she caught me with my trousers down,' he explained. 'I had to think quick, so I taul her I was researching a new business venture.

'After I got out of hospital I came up with Prodhub, a wabsite that is wall-to-wall filth for people who don't like sex.'

We gained exclusive early access to the site and were literally unshocked at its content.

Viewers can watch videos of all kinds of non-sexual activities, including well stacked mounds of fresh traybakes being salaciously eaten in church halls, couples driving to Portrush before having a poke in a lay-by, and a clip entitled 'contentious root' which shows a band parade in Rasharkin.

Most shockingly of all, there's a section devoted to swingers. Bondage appears to be involved, as they're all chained up on a Sunday.

If successful in this venture Mr Oldman intends to launch a site for 'themuns'.

'It consists entirely of videos of men in tight shorts playing with their balls,' he told us. 'Hopefully it'll go down well in the GAA community.'

Civil servant executed after failing to adhere to GDPR guidelines

A Belfast civil servant has become the first person in Europe to be executed under the EU's stringent new General Data Protection Regulations (GDPR).

It is understood that twenty-eight-year-old Mal Ware left his desk at the Department of Agriculture, Environment, and Rural Affairs (DAIRRHEA) at eleven o'clock this morning. He was immediately arrested.

'The culprit failed to delete an email containing sensitive data,' said Inspector Rex El-Spreadsheet from the EU cyber-security division. 'On closer examination this was found to contain several information identifiers, including the name, address and telephone number of a private individual.'

Mr Ware pleaded innocence, pointing out that the offending email was his own holiday booking and that he was the individual in question, but his protests were rejected.

'If that information had fallen into the wrong hands, someone could have done something,' explained the official.

Mr Ware was immediately taken to Stormont Castle where he was sentenced to death and executed by firing squad.

'We'd hoped to use a guillotine,' we were told by a DAIRRHEA spokesman, 'but the one in the office wasn't big enough.'

Artist's Impression

99

The Hosepipe Ban
HOW TO SAVE WATER

 Flush the toilet as litte as possible: Remember the rule – if it's yellow, let it mellow, if it's brown, flush it down.

 In fact scrap that, don't use the toilet at all. If you need to go, pish in your garden. If you don't have a garden, pish in someone else's.

 Only use beer to water plants. Plants like beer and we think it kills slugs or something.

 Beer is also an excellent replacement for drinking water. Stay drunk at all times.

 Don't have showers. Just plaster yourself in Lynx Africa. Soon enough everyone will be stinkin anyway, and you'll be too drunk to notice.

 Don't bother washing your car either. Just spray it with Lynx as well, at least it'll smell nice .

HOW MANY NORN IRON POLITICIANS DOES IT TAKE TO CHANGE A LIGHTBULB?

	Alliance	NI Conservatives
The bulb should be replaced under a grant funded scheme which pays users to switch it on.	The lightbulb can choose if and when it wishes to change and everyone must accept its chosen off/on designation.	Don't Unionist and Nationalist lightbulbs in Northern Ireland help change each other?
	 Sinn Féin	UUP
The lightbulb must be forcibly removed and sent back to its country of origin	This lightbulb has 15 minutes to get out.	The lightbulb still has a lot to offer voters though it hasn't had any power for ages.
greenparty	SDLP	traditional unionist voice
This bulb is environmentally unsound and must be replaced with an ethical light source made out of hemp.	This lightbulb is enshrined under the Good Friday Agreement and cannot be changed	CHANGE? NEVER! NEVER! NEVER! NEVER!

Sammy Wilson disproves existence of God', say theologians

A gathering of religious thinkers has accepted that the existence of Sammy Wilson means that it is 'highly unlikely' there is any kind of supreme creator in Heaven.

Leaders from all the main world religions attended the meeting, which was held in a large tent near Lisburn. After several days of heated debate they were forced to admit that no rational, intelligent God would ever allow Mr Wilson to be elected as an MP.

'It would seem we've been asking the wrong questions for centuries,' said the Archbishop of Canterbury. 'We've wondered – why does God allow war and suffering? Or – why did God create disease?

'We've ignored the biggest question of all – how in the name of all that is holy does an arsehole like that get to be in a position of importance in society?'

The news has also forced an urgent rethink by scientists, who are now reconsidering their theories on the formation of the universe.

'The Big Bang Theory would appear to be out of date,' said Professor Brian Cox, who is the only scientist we know, now that Stephen Hawking is dead.

'We're working on the "Big Arse Theory" instead. So far we've discovered that if you take a standard horse's arse and a baboon's big red one and fire them into each other in that Large Hadron Collider yoke, you get something that closely resembles Sammy Wilson when they explode.'

We approached God for comment but a spokesangel told us that he was too busy moving in mysterious ways.

'Yer hole, we'll have our own World Cup,' says whole of Ireland

With both Northern Ireland and the Republic exiting the World Cup at the final hurdle, the IFA and FAI have finally got together and agreed to hold their own 'All Ireland' tournament next year.

It is understood that the associations intend to field sixteen sides each, so that they'll be able to play each other multiple times and complete a full tournament.

All retired international players have been recalled to active service and the search is already on to find thirty-two different managers who have the surname O'Neill. The eligible players will then be divided into age categories to ensure a level playing field.

'It's gonna be a fairly complex draw,' admitted a senior IFA spokesman. 'We'll not only need to make sure there are two teams from each association in every group of four, we also have to avoid a situation where Pat Jennings leads the Northern Ireland over-70s against the Republic's under-21s.

FIFA WORLD CUP
Ireland 2018

'Although to be honest I still reckon we'd win.'

Fans of both teams have welcomed the move. 'It'll be mighty craic altogether,' we were told by one Republic fan from Lurgan. 'Sure this way we're guaranteed to get to the final, and we can all get blocked for the whole tournament.'

Fresh from his insightful article on *Belfast Live* today, local journalist and football expert Joe Lindsay is understood to be looking forward to the tournament, and is planning to write a series of articles without actually attending any matches.

Bonfires are for arseholes, reveal scientists

A new study conducted by an international team of scientists has concluded that the annual Northern Irish ritual of setting fire to things is mainly enjoyed by arseholes.

'It's clear that building huge pyres with pallets and bedecking them with the symbols of your neighbours before burning them is not the behaviour of rational thinkers,' said the report's author, Professor Fu Keen Obvious. 'It's more likely to be arseholes.'

The report follows another evening of embarrassment in Derry, where, not content with spending much of the summer trying to set fire to the Fountain Estate, local youths burned a load of things they'd nicked from it instead.

The usual spiral of whataboutery on Twitter followed, with supporters pointing out that nationalist symbols were burned in the Fountain and other loyalist areas in July. 'It's easy to deal with this type of debate,' says the professor, 'if you accept that arseholery is one of our few cross-community activities.'

Politicians were quick to condemn the bonfire, claiming that it was unrepresentative of the local community.

'No one here wants this, not even the people who lined up to watch it,' said Sinn Féin MLA Barry O'Hara, who hasn't been at work for nearly two years so has managed to avoid doing anything about the problem.

However local bonfire builder John Vesta defended the display. 'I regard it as a form of protest art designed to commemorate the Assumption of the Virgin Mary,' he told us. 'Even adding poppy wreaths and the names of murdered members of the security forces – that's all cultural and stuff.'

We tried to contact the Virgin Mary for comment but she wasn't in the phone book. However she later appeared in a vision and told us that everyone involved was an arsehole.

Catholic church announces St Tropez as patron saint of fake tan

Pope Francis has revealed that St Tropez will in future be known as the patron saint of people who smear themselves in chemicals in an attempt to look like they come from California.

We bumped into the Pontiff outside the Europa Hotel, where he was handing out leaflets advertising his summer tour of Ireland.

'It is time that we recognised the contribution of some of the lesser-known saints,' Mr Francis explained. 'I mean, you've got yer big hitters, Patrick, Peter, Paul, Percy, but what about the rest of them? They do a key job in being patronising on a daily basis.

'Just the other day I was in Dunnes Stores, buying a nice maroon jumper, when I clocked the label and suddenly thought to myself, when was the last time anyone asked you to pray to St Bernard, the patron saint of reasonably priced knitwear?

'I thought for a while, then remembered – it was 1984, when I was a poor priest just out of the seminary. All I've done since is pay homage to St Michael, round the corner in Marks and Spencer.'

The move will be made official at a special service when the Pope makes his visit to Ireland this summer, with several famous devotees expected to be in attendance, including David Dickinson, Christine Bleakley and Barra Best.

All teenage girls from Derry have been given the day off in honour of the occasion.

Surviving Brexit
Official Government Guidance.

Department for Exiting the European Union

PROTECT AND SURVIVE

This booklet tells you how to make your home and your family as safe as possible under Brexit

---

1. Build a migrant shelter

---

2. Stockpile alcohol

The best way to survive Brexit is to get totally plastered. Make homebrew in the bath.

---

3. Food

The only food available after Brexit will be proper British food, none of that foreign muck. Prepare your family by avoiding that foreign muck in the months ahead. Then stockpile proper British food as well, because to be fair we'll probably run out inside a week.

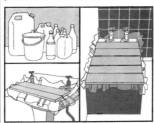

---

4. Clothes

The only clothing acceptable after Brexit will be good old British clothes from the 70s - like parka coats, Pringle sweaters and leather driving gloves. Anyone seen wearing any of that fancy European fashion will be deported to its country of origin.

Other useful things

5. Bedding: for some reason.

6. A portable stove, for when the gas runs out

7. Torches etc as there'll be no electric (That's probably why you need bedding as well)

8. £350 million for the NHS.

9. Stuff to make a toilet (see10. Sanitation).

---

10. Sanitation

You will spend much of your time in the post Brexit era shitting yourself. Make a toilet in the living room so you can still see the TV.

Use a chair from the 1970s as a seat, and a bucket with a plastic liner.

Don't forget to wipe your arse afterwards. Europe isn't there to do it for you now.

---

11. The Irish Border

If you're unlucky enough to live in Northern Ireland, we haven't a clue what we'll do with you afterwards to be honest. However if you find yourself in the Republic on Brexit Day, run to the nearest British Embassy and wait for the helicopters to arrive to take you home.

If you're in the countryside, crawl along in a ditch til you see a big orange glow in the sky. That means you've made it to Portadown and you're safe.

---

12. Remember the warning sounds

THE BREXIT WARNING

When Brexit is expected, the sirens will sound a rising and falling note, like a long fart.

THE FALL OUT WARNING

When the post-Brexit fallout kicks in, you will hear three loud bangs in succession. That'll be Cameron, Johnson and Farage being shot

THE ALL CLEAR

We wouldn't worry about this one, you'll be dead by the time it's sounded.

Controversy as Ballyhackamore named 'Town most up its own hole' 2018

There was sporadic complaining on the streets of Hillsborough this afternoon as the East Belfast district of Ballyhackamore was controversially crowned 'Town most up its own hole', despite not actually being a town.

The news was also greeted with dismay by residents of finalists Holywood, Moira and Glenarm, but the judging panel has explained that the category of 'town' has been expanded for 2018.

'It's quite clear that the people of Ballyhackamore have been working hard to be up their own holes for years,' said Head Judge Sir Horatio Todd. 'It seemed so unfair to leave out somewhere with so many restaurants that seat you at old school desks and serve tiny portions of tapas on gigantic wooden platters made out of recycled shipwreck timber.'

Ballyhackamore resident Camilla Campbell-Campbell admitted that she was a bit surprised. 'We're not really a town, are we? There's more of a village feel here. But it is a wonderful place to live. We're so close to the city centre, which would be so convenient if we had to travel there, but I work from home as a part-time artisan fashion blogger and my husband Campbell makes environmentally-sourced beard wax in the shed.'

Local vinyl-record dealer Brett Rofurniture agreed. 'I don't think we're up our own holes – we're just more enlightened than everyone else.

'We're so welcoming in "The Hack". Literally anyone can move here, if they can afford £300 grand for a two-bedroom semi with a box room.'

BREAKING NEWS: It has emerged that Bangor has launched a legal challenge against the result, and police have arrested three people in Crawfordsburn for sending a strongly worded email to the judges.

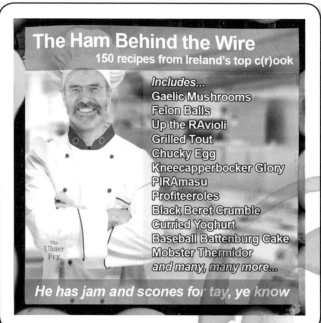

The Ham Behind the Wire
150 recipes from Ireland's top c(r)ook

Includes...
Gaelic Mushrooms
Felon Balls
Up the RAvioli
Grilled Tout
Chucky Egg
Kneecapperbocker Glory
PIRAmasu
Profiteeroles
Black Beret Crumble
Curried Yoghurt
Baseball Battenburg Cake
Mobster Thermidor
and many, many more...

The Ulster Fry

He has jam and scones for tay, ye know

How much do you need a good boot up the hole?

Have you ever wondered whether you need a good boot up the hole? Of course you have.

Luckily the psychologists at Fivemiletown University have been looking into this eternal question, and have come up with a handy test to help you find out.

1. How do you talk into a mobile phone?

A. Quietly, holding it to my ear.

B. On a hands-free, so I look like I'm talking to myself in the street.

C. I shout loudly while holding it away from my face, like I'm on *The Apprentice*.

2. What kind of drinks do you order in pubs?

A. Just pints or bottled beer. Maybe a glass of wine with a meal and the occasional short (but only with one mixer).

B. Pretty much the same as A, but the odd time I might order a hot whiskey so the barman has to faff around with kettles.

C. Extremely complicated cocktails that take ages to make so that no one else can get served.

3. Assuming you're a grown-up, would you ever consider using a skateboard?

A. No, they're for weans.

B. I might if I was playing with the kids.

C. I travel to work on one every day, even though I'm in my early 30s and should know better.

4. Would you ever take your shoes off in work?

A. Never. No one should be barefoot in work except folk in the Olympics and maybe those masseurs who walk up and down your back.

B. Maybe, if my shoes got very wet.

C. Every day, I enjoy the feel of dirty carpet under my feet and I'm a complete pervert.

5. When driving, how often do you indicate?

A. Always.

B. Usually but I mightn't bother if there's no one else around.

C. Never. I own the road and you scumbags just have to guess where I'm going.

6. How many tattoos do you have?

A. None.

B. Just a wee discreet one on my shoulder.

C. All my limbs are plastered in Maori body art even though I'm from Newtownstewart.

7. How much stuff do you buy in petrol stations?

A. Petrol or diesel, and a can of Lilt if I'm thirsty.

B. Same as A, but maybe a loaf or milk if I run out through the week.

C. My entire weekly shop. I load up two trolleys and then try to pay using a whole rake of out-of-date vouchers I cut out of the paper before forgetting my PIN number and writing a cheque.

How did you get on?

Score 0 points for every A, 5 points for every B and 10 points for a C.

0–10 points: Your arse is safe.

10–25 points: You're borderline, the occasional fly kick may be needed.

25–50 points: Time to invest in a pair of steel underpants.

50 and above: You should never be able to sit down again.

'Protestants make the best traybakes,' admits Pope

Centuries of religious conflict came to an end last night when Pope Francis made the startling admission that Protestant churches serve a more impressive array of baked goods than their Catholic counterparts.

In an exclusive interview with *The Ulster Fry*, the Pontiff explained that Vatican historians have been studying the works of Martin Luther, and have decided that he may have had a point after all.

'It seems that when he nailed his 95 theses to that door in Wittenberg, it was actually a list of traybake recipes that would have revolutionised religious catering forever.

'We could have been eating delicious things like Fifteens, Caramel Squares, Rocky Roads and Flies' Graveyards – instead we were stuck with the Diet of Worms.'*

* Winner of the most of obscure religious joke competition 1964

Pope Francis now intends to reach out the hand of friendship to Protestant church leaders. 'I kinda hope they'll put a Coconut Slice in it,' he confessed.

The revelation has been met with a conciliatory response.

'To be fair, Catholics have better wakes,' said the Queen, who is head of the Church of England in her spare time. 'When my ma died, she lay in state for a lock of days. If we'd been Catholics we could have all been drinking cans of Harp in the kitchen till the funeral.'

Whoever the Moderator of the Presbyterian Church is agreed. 'Catholics have far better craic at church,' he said. 'All that standing up and sitting down stuff beats sitting on your hole listening to some eejit talking about hell for two hours. *And* they have bingo.'

As a result of the discussion there is now only one church for everyone, the Queen and the Pope have swapped jobs, and a team of Free Presbyterians from County Down will be playing a home fixture against Tyrone at the Edward Carson Gaelic Athletic Club in Annahilt.

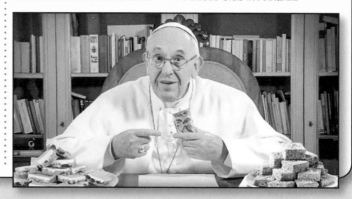

The Ulster Fry

No Beans

Sinn Féin to offer new range of 'coaching' services

With Sinn Féin embroiled in controversy over their alleged coaching of 'loyalist blogger' Jamie Bryson for a Stormont Committee, *The Ulster Fry* can exclusively reveal that this is just a small part of their plan to enter the lucrative coaching business on a more permanent basis.

An insider told us that given that working with someone like Bryson clearly wasn't a problem, then they'd be quite prepared to put aside whatever principles they have if it would benefit them in some way.

Here's a few options.

Coach hire

An obvious choice, so obvious we didn't even have to Photoshop. The new Sinn Féin bus service – dubbed the Contentious Routemaster – will operate on both sides of the border. However the chances are you'll share your journey with a few cattle and a barrel or two of laundered diesel.

Sports Coaching...................................

All manner of sports will be on offer – shooting, baseball, (gun) running and political football to name but a few.

Life Coaching...

Or how to do a stretch in prison. The perpetually smiling Martina Anderson seems like the obvious contender to lead these classes, though she mightn't like the colour of the jumpsuit.

Irish Language Coaching........................

Gerry is widely acknowledged in Sinn Féin circles as THE master of the Irish Language. His new night classes in Connolly House are bound to be an attraction.

Voice Coaching.......................................

After many years of being dubbed on the news, the Shinners should be well set to act as voice coaches for aspiring actors or singers. Who better to fulfil this role than the ever so articulate Barry McElduff?

 If all else fails, they can always fall back on politics. There's always a pound or two in that racket.

NI charities rebrand as terror groups to improve funding chances

As the scandal grows over the handling of the Social Investment Fund in Northern Ireland, several charities and community groups here are sensationally set to reposition themselves as terror groups in a bid to get better funding.

'We heard all the craic today on *Nolan*,' said Toby Pencil from the now defunct NI Guide Dog Association. 'It's beginning to feel like it's easier to get your hands on public money if you're a front for some kind of paramilitary group, so we're going to try it the other way round.

'We're rebranding as the Irish National Labradoration Army from tomorrow, and training all our dogs to covertly crap on public pavements. We'll be making shitloads in no time!'

This is a view shared by Gerry Hatrick from the newly formed Lisburn Pensioners' Aid. 'We put in an application for help with a "meals-on-wheels" service a while ago but heard nothing back. This time round we've booby-trapped the van. Maybe they'll listen now.'

Meanwhile, in East Belfast, a shadowy group called the Real Ulster Volunteer Force has been touring the area actually doing voluntary work. 'We'll probably have to deal drugs the odd time to maintain our cover,' said sixty-seven-year-old Brigadier Sammy Handyman, 'but we'll try and keep it to Calpol and Feminax.'

However one local charity is refusing to change its name.

Sure we've been at this carry-on for years. I'm surprised it took so long for the rest to catch on,' said Major Ivan Trumpet from the Salvation Army.

Everyone's faith in politics here restored, says grateful electorate

The people of Northern Ireland are united in praise of their political representatives this evening after another day of edifying shenanigans at Stormont.

The day began with a number of walkouts, swiftly followed by a statement from the First Minister – which wasn't a First Minister's statement – delivered to an empty chamber. She then answered some probing questions from her own MLAs before everyone broke for lunch.

The afternoon session was an even more stunning demonstration of democracy in action. The MLAs who had walked out walked back in to listen to a different statement from the same First Minister, there were some angry exchanges and eventually a vote of no confidence, that failed, despite gaining a majority of votes.

Many voters we spoke to declared themselves 'delighted' with the performance.

'I'm delighted with the performance,' said Bangor man Cole Sacks, as he waited in traffic gridlock on part of our utterly inadequate transport network. 'It's good to see that our leaders managed to squeeze in a crisis before the end of the year. They were nearly out of time, but you can always count on them to find some banal shite to make a bollocks of.'

'Great work on the Hill,' exclaimed thirty-four-year-old Olly Fill. 'Apparently they were meant to be agreeing on the budget today, but that kind of thing can wait.

'When I got that redundancy notice yesterday, I said just the same thing to the wife about starting a family.'

Meanwhile, at Stormont, everyone is congratulating themselves on another successful day spent running the country.

'School Assembly' to replace Stormont in radical shake-up

As arguments rage over the latest Stormont crisis, the British and Irish governments have stunned political observers by replacing the Assembly with a random selection of small children from local primary schools, in the vague hope that they might actually start getting something done.

The new 'School Assembly' took over the reins of government this morning, and immediately set about choosing an executive to take control of the various departments. 'We chose Jack to be First Minister,' said six-year-old Chloe, Chairgirl of the Agriculture Committee, 'cos he is the tallest and can run really, really fast in races and he can sit on people.'

Jack's best friend Michael has been installed as Deputy First Minister. 'We've made Jessica from Mrs Kelly's class the Finance one,' said Michael. 'She is the best at sums and can count backwards from a hundred. Wayne will do Justice cos he has a cowboy suit with a sheriff's badge and everything. Sarah is being arts and stuff cos she doesn't go over the lines when she colours in.'

We understand that other ministerial positions were likewise filled 'on merit', although the appointment of the new Communities Minister was decided 'by a farting competition' – the same method used in selecting the previous post holder Paul Givan.

As of six o'clock this evening, the children had agreed a solution to the health crisis, with seven-year-old minister Amanda Brown telling reporters that queues at A&E would be slashed because 'you're only allowed to see the nurse if you're sick.'

The flags and parades issue has also been resolved and investment is being sought to improve transport, with new rail links served by large-faced steam engines singled out as a number one priority.

Sadly, however, there was little progress on the RHI inquiry, with ministers unable to reach agreement on whether to use Chinese burns or 'diddy nips' to get people to talk.

Liam Neeson urged to run for First Minister

Hollywood superstar Liam Neeson has been urged to come home and sort the country out today, after a video appeared online in which he appears to make perfect sense, doesn't repeatedly blame themuns or show anyone in their pyjamas.

Mr Neeson is backing a campaign to replace Northern Ireland's popular segregated education system, which has successfully taught children how to get along with their 'own sort' for generations – with a new-fangled 'integrated' approach, in which kids as young as four years old will be controversially expected to make friends of all religions.

'I'd vote for big Liam any day of the week,' said Belfast woman Ann Square. 'He's been a Jedi, King Aslan and Zeus, twice, so he's well used to positions of power. Plus remember the time he sorted out an angry pack of wolves with his bare hands whilst pure foundered? Our lot would be wee buns for him.'

The news has been criticised by the DUP, however, who say his role as Michael Collins in the 1996 biopic would never be forgotten by unionist voters, whilst his appearance in *Love Actually*, which they admittedly haven't even seen, did sound 'a bit gay'.

Sinn Féin have meanwhile said his role as the Bad Cop in 2014's *Lego Movie* was 'concerning' to nationalist voters, and questioned whether there was any RUC involvement.

The video is online … have a look, if ye are into that whole 'getting along' thing.

DUP unveil Trump-like travel ban for Northern Ireland

With scandal engulfing the United States following Donald Trump's travel ban, the DUP today unveiled an updated election manifesto that proposes a similar scheme in Northern Ireland.

'The first country we'll ban will be the Republic of Ireland of course,' revealed Arlene Foster earlier. 'We're not sure how hard the border can become after Brexit, but our engineers are looking at several options, including reinforced concrete, steel, titanium and dried-in Weetabix.

'Next up, anyone from the Ivory Coast won't be allowed in,' she continued. 'We simply can't take the risk they'd bring a flag with them. One wrong turn and we'd have another tricolour flying on our streets. It's too big a security risk.'

Other countries on the proposal include the Dominican Republic and the People's Republic of Congo. 'Mostly cos they have "Republic" in their name,' explained Foster. 'But also cos I knew a fella called Dominic once – and he was a dick.

'Also, I hate Um Bongo,' she added.

Unlike the US ban, the NI version is not just aimed at nations with primarily Muslim populations. However, there are two notable exceptions.

'It goes without saying that our borders would be closed

to anyone from Iraq or Iran,' added Foster finally. 'You can't seriously expect the name of your country to be "IRA" with another wee letter just slapped on the end,' she said. 'It's an absolute disgrace in this day and age.'

Reports suggesting the Iranian president will change his country's name to 'Udan' so he can continue holidaying in Portrush remain unconfirmed.

Gerry Adams gets rousing reception as he launches DUP election manifesto

Gerry Adams was the surprise guest at today's DUP election manifesto launch, and was greeted warmly by the party faithful.

'Thank God you're here,' North Belfast MP Nigel Dodds was heard to whisper to the former Sinn Féin president. 'We thought we were on a hiding to nothing in this election, what with all that RHI stuff floating about. Then it occurred to us, let's wheel out Gerry to scare the bejaysus out of the masses.'

The bearded republican was given a hearty welcome by DUP leader Arlene Foster, whose speech served as a warm-up act for her republican opponent.

'You'll all know the man I'm about to introduce,' she told her audience, while her surprise guest loomed in the shadows waiting for his star turn. 'He's been knocking around the political circuit here for years, serving his time with some of the greats – and now he's very kindly agreed to come along here today to help us get this show on the road.'

Mr Adams then took centre stage and went through a range of his most famous impressions – including Fungus

the Bogeyman, Frankenstein's monster and the Creature from the Black Lagoon – sending the DUP's supporters into paroxysms of fear.

'This is just what we came for,' Councillor Walter McIlrobinson told us as he changed his underpants. 'No one gives me the election willies more than thon auld fecker, and I've had more election willies put up me than I care to remember.'

Following the launch the assembled throng made their way to a nearby church hall for light refreshments, with entertainment provided by Ballymoney hip-hop act, MC Rea and the Renewable Beat Incentive.

Arlene Foster injured by elephant during DUP trip to the circus

DUP leader Arlene Foster suffered minor injuries this afternoon in what has been described as a 'freak accident' during a visit to the circus with party colleagues.

It is understood that Mrs Foster had taken MPs Jeffrey Donaldson and Gavin Robinson on the trip in a bid to cheer them up after last week's election.

'Wee Jeffrey and Gavin were very upset about Friday's results so Arlene thought she'd treat them, even though it's a Sunday,' we were told by a senior DUP source. 'It started well enough: she bought them both candyfloss and they really enjoyed the clowns, but it all went wrong during a photo shoot with one of the elephants.

'Something must have spooked it, and next thing it reared up and started charging. Jeffrey and Gavin made a run for it and shouted at Arlene to get out of the way, but she just stood there and the thing ran straight over her. Fortunately

she landed in a large deposit of elephant dung on the ring's floor so avoided serious injury.'

Mrs Foster's refusal to step aside has been described as 'bizarre' by eyewitnesses. 'If she'd just listened to common sense and got out of the way for a bit, she could have avoided being trampled in shite for no good reason,' we were told by one acrobat.

This is not the first time that the DUP leader's intransigence has caused her problems. In 2015 she caused a forty-person pile up by refusing to step aside during a line dancing session in Kesh Orange Hall.

Gerry Adams to let Michelle O'Neill speak as International Women's Day gesture

Following a series of embarrassing media engagements yesterday in which Michelle O'Neill kept her trap shut so the big man could speak, Gerry Adams today revealed plans to let her actually say stuff in celebration of International Women's Day (IWD).

'I think it's important that we mark the valuable contribution women have made in our society,' began Adams at Sinn Féin's IWD press launch earlier. 'So today you're going to be hearing from one of the brightest and most capable female politicians of our era, whom I recently appointed to lead Sinn Féin in Northern Ireland.'

'Auch, thanks Gerry, that's really kind of y—'

'Sorry, Michelle, if you'd just let me finish, one wee second …' interrupted Adams.

'Anyway, as I was saying, I think it's really important that we recognise the role Michelle played in our recent election success, and continues to play

in the ongoing talks in Stormont, in which I've also played a minor role, making key decisions and speaking to the press on her behalf,' he continued … for about 35 minutes.

'Aye, what he said,' added O'Neill afterwards.

World of social media reacts predictably to death of Martin McGuinness

As the news of the passing of Martin McGuinness broke on mainstream media, Northern Ireland's assortment of keyboard commentators took to their smartphones to add their usual considered opinions.

Facebook user 'Ballybeen Bear', who served eight years for arms offences in the 1980s, was quick to highlight the former Deputy First Minister's IRA past. 'Forty years too late,' he commented on the *Belfast Telegraph*'s article.

Elsewhere, others described Mr McGuinness as

a saint, comparing him to Nelson Mandela, Jesus and Gandhi rolled into one. 'People criticising his past need to be more respectful,' replied @Pearse1916, who had previously tweeted 'Ding dong the witch is dead' when Margaret Thatcher died.

Others adopted a more biblical tone. 'Vengeance is mine, I will repay, says the Lord, *Romans 12:19*,' tweeted @luther1517 who conveniently appears to have forgotten 'Judge not, that ye be not judged, *Matthew 7:1*.'

Elsewhere, half-normal people were digesting the news of the passing of someone who, like him or not, was undoubtedly a key figure in the peace process.

'Both the Chuckle Brothers are gone now, at a time when it might be handy to have them around,' commented Facebook user Helena Hancart. 'They might do a better job than the Scissor Sisters.'

'We can't be arsed with another election, now sort it out you ballbags,' everyone tells MLAs, in long headline shock

The Northern Ireland political parties have been sent a very clear message this morning after *The Ulster Fry* was forced to write a really long headline about the talks process.

'We've only been running for two and a half years,' said a spokesman for the funny/unfunny* website, 'and we've had two Assembly elections,

* delete as applicable

a Westminster election, a council election and the Brexit referendum. We really don't want to have to think up stupid ideas for another one in May.'

The revelation comes after Sinn Féin told everyone that they couldn't be bothered continuing with the talks. Speaking through Michelle O'Neill, Gerry Adams told reporters that they wouldn't be nominating anyone as Speaker of the Assembly 'because, that's why'.

DUP leader Arlene Foster insisted that Sinn Féin are to blame. 'They think their mandate is the only one that matters,' she explained, 'when in fact ours is.'

The collapse of the talks leaves Northern Ireland without a budget and with no effective response to Brexit, although Secretary of State James Brokenshite told us that 'the sun's out, so it's not all bad'.

While everyone agrees that the sun being out is 'a good thing', it also seems like a good idea to have the Assembly back to do its traditional half-arsed job of running the country, since at present there appears to be a no-arsed approach to government.

However at time of publication no one can be arsed.

DUP and Sinn Féin agree shock General Election pact

Northern Ireland's two main parties have surprised experts by agreeing to work together to maximise their support in June's snap General Election.

It is understood that Gerry Adams met Arlene Foster for top secret talks at an undisclosed location in County Fermanagh. Mr Adams later denied being at the meeting although this means that it must have happened, probably twice.

As a result of the talks Mrs Foster has agreed to be as obnoxious possible towards nationalists, while Mr Adams has assured the DUP leader that he'll make vaguely threatening speeches and keep going on about a border poll in order to wind up unionists.

According to seasoned political analyst Newton Hamilton, this tactic has worked before. 'Sure we saw how successfully Mrs Foster got the Sinn Féin vote out in the last Assembly election,' he told us, 'and the "Gerry-act-trick" always works a treat for the DUP.

'Basically this election won't be about fancy things like health, education or even Brexit, it'll be about counting how many of usuns and themuns there are, as usual.'

In a related story, both parties have begun frantic campaigns to get as many voters registered as possible, with observers reporting long queues of party activists outside cemeteries across the Province.

'I don't normally do elections but this one seems dead important, although at my age I'll have to get a postal vote,' said the newly registered Charity McAlpine, who according to her gravestone turned 142 on her last birthday.

Controversial 'English Language Act' proposed for Northern Ireland

The debate around Northern Ireland's linguistic culture took an unusual twist today with the launch of a campaign for an English Language Act specifically tailored for the Province.

The move comes from the Belfast Area Royal Society for English Speakers, a new organisation dedicated to promoting the language across Northern Ireland.

'The English language is now virtually extinct in many places,' said BareaRSES chairman Dr Johnson Samuel. 'It has reached the stage where it is almost impossible to understand what anyone in North Antrim is saying, not that you'd really want to, and don't get me started on the Derry wans.'

Under the terms of the proposed act, employers would be legally obliged to use English when dealing with customers, with local council language officers enforcing the legislation.

'It's very simple,' says Dr Samuel. 'Instead of a shop assistant saying *D'ye wanna wee beg wi' lat*, they would ask *Would you like a carrier bag?*, and *Are you gittin'?* would be replaced with *Are you being served?*'

The proposal produced a furious reaction on social media with self-employed part-time mad bastard Glen Gormley summing up the feelings of many people in an angry Facebook post.

'Wat r thesuns on abt intreferin in or way off talkin here they can fuk of back to England or wereva there from the bastards.'

If adopted, it is understood that the act would be trialled in Belfast then extended to cover the rest of Northern Ireland.

'Except Tyrone,' says Dr Samuel. 'It's a lost cause.'

Northern Ireland set to elect its first 'openly sectarian' MP

Following the news that the Republic has an openly gay taoiseach, it has emerged that voters in Northern Ireland are on the verge of electing the first MP here to openly admit that he's a bigoted bastard.

Whilst there is a long history of electing sectarian hurbags in the Province, such MPs generally try and dress up their bigotry by claiming that they'll 'represent all their constituents without fear or favour', but this year the East Tyrone constituency brings together two candidates who can't be arsed with such charades.

'I f**king hate Fenians,' admitted DUP candidate Carson Williamson-Williamson. 'If I had my way they'd all be shipped down south, soap-dodging bastards that they are, but not before I organise a Lambeg drumming match in each and every one of their gardens and give them an individually-tailored boot up the hole.'

Meanwhile Sinn Féin candidate Padraig Sands-Connolly-Pearse told us he hoped that a border poll would bring about an Ireland of equals.

'One that equals all the Huns f**king back home to England. Jaffa bastards.

'Let's not beat about the bush here: our policy is to make this place as unpleasant as possible for the f**kers and eventually they'll all piss off.'

Fortunately both politicians do agree on some key issues.

'If we both work together we can keep the political pot boiling and everyone will keep voting for our parties,' they told us, separately.

London Hipster 'hated the DUP before it was cool'

A Shoreditch hipster has claimed to be the first person in the country to think that the DUP are a bunch of arseholes, it has emerged.

Twenty-five-year-old Peckham Market told us that he'd Googled the DUP 'ages ago'.

'Yeah, like, I'd been doing some research about the election on Saturday – in this really hip cafe that serves artisan food on plates made out of beard shavings – and I was like "whoaa, these guys are way uncool". I mean, they're into some kind of religion that isn't ethnic.

'So I made a podcast about it, telling all my followers how uncool they are. And they're all like – "OMG! These guys are so intolerant. They can't think for themselves like we can. Thanks for telling us, Peckham."

'And it's not like I don't know about the Troubles and stuff, you know? I read an article about it all in the *Guardian*.

'I'm thinking of organising a protest. You guys really should stop fighting and try real politics, like we have here.'

Mr Market, who runs a micro-brewery making craft ale infused with Haribo, is the son of Sir Camden Market, the former Conservative MP for Little Skidmark-on-the-Hole.

'The DUP ate my hamster,' claims family man

The DUP's image in the UK was further tarnished today, after party leader Arlene Foster was accused of eating a family's pet hamster amid ongoing talks with the Conservative Party.

'She landed in our house the other day slabbering that she was "top dog now" and demanding that us "peasants" make her tea and biscuits,' alleged thirty-eight year-old Peterborough dad, Peter Borough. 'Poor wee Elmo didn't take her on, God bless him, but when Arlene noticed him running on his wheel, on a Sunday, she totally lost the plot! Snatched him right out of his cage and literally ate the bake off him.

'She was rambling on about him being a "hateful sinner". But her mouth was full to be fair,' he admitted, 'so she might have said "shinner".

'How this DUP crowd claim to be truly British like us is beyond me, though,' he sobbed. 'Cos she didn't even dunk him into her tea or anything.'

The unconfirmed news comes after several days of intense criticism of the DUP in which the party has been publicly lambasted for a litany of heinous acts including homophobia, Islamophobia, arachnophobia, leaving the immersion heater on, double parking, not indicating at roundabouts, listening to Nickelback, enjoying televised snooker and downloading Songs of Praise from an illegal torrent site, amongst others.

'We refute these ridiculous accusations,' said DUP spokesman Chip Monkstown. 'But to save any further arguments, I've got a new hamster being delivered today, just for them.

'The pet shop boys should coming in my back door any minute now,' he added.

Talks drag on to allow parties to spend more time in new Stormont hot tub

The Stormont talks are likely to last at least another twenty-four hours after it emerged that Theresa May had bought the DUP a state-of-the-art hot tub as part of their Westminster deal.

The Ulster Fry understands that the facility has been installed in a new beer garden to the rear of Parliament Buildings, alongside a bouncy castle. 'That's for the younger MLAs,' a senior civil servant revealed, 'and Gavin Robinson.'

'It's class,' we were told by veteran Shinner Gerry Adams. 'Me and Arlene have been in there all morning. My ballsack has more wrinkles than a forged electoral ID in Foyle, but I'm for staying in as long as possible.'

Mrs Foster explained that the purchase of the hot tub was actually a serious attempt to get the talks process moving.

'We're not just sitting up here taking the pish – that would be unhygienic for a start,' she argued. 'We fully intend to work through all the issues in a thorough and methodical manner

'A few glasses of champagne and a game of "catch the floating voter" along the way can hardly hurt,' she continued.

Politicians in the other devolved regions are said to be furious that the Tories have given Northern Ireland such an apparently generous deal.

'This is a blatant attempt to purchase votes. We get nothing here,' said the SNP's Angus Sourbake, after he returned home from the launch of a f*cking huge aircraft carrier in Fife.

10 per cent of civil servants will have to phone in sick using Irish, claim Language Act opponents

Sinn Féin have rubbished claims that 10 per cent of new entrants to the Civil Service will have to phone in sick in Irish if their proposed Language Act becomes law.

'This is ridiculous,' said former Sinn Féin President Gerry Adams. 'Even fluent speakers like me can't say diarrhoea in Irish, and I am famous for my ability to talk shite. Obviously the three thousand new Irish-speaking civil servants (that we aren't demanding) will be able to phone in using English, just like the lesser mortals.'

Despite his claims, we thought it'd be useful for *The Ulster Fry* to come up with a few handy phrases to help new recruits get around the proposed 'Gaelige Sickie Act'. Obviously we had to use Google Translate, so apologies to anyone whose Irish skills are better than Gerry's.

Tá an shite ag rith amach glan dom: The shite is running clean out of me.

Na snatters ag tripping mé, ionas go bhfuil siad: The snatters are tripping me, so they are.

Ní raibh tú a fheiceáil dom sa teach tábhairne, caithfidh sé a bheith ar mo cúpla: You did not see me in the pub, it must have been my twin.

Casacht, casacht: Cough, cough.

Caithfidh sé a bheith rud éigin a ith mé: It must have been something I ate.

Mo sheanmháthair fuair bás: My granny died.

Cad atá i gceist agat, Sin mo thríú granny i mí?: What do you mean, that's my third granny in a month?

DUP MP Sammy Wilson washed away in floods

Prominent DUP MP Sammy Wilson and his views on climate change have been completely washed away in last night's flooding, a party spokesman has admitted.

The Ulster Fry understands that the East Antrim representative's flood defences were finally breached by a torrent of water at 9 p.m. last night, with satellite images showing him floating northwards off the coast of Scotland.

'Sammy has traditionally relied on making stuff up as his defence in the climate change debate,' we were told by the DUP insider. 'Sadly we'll now have to admit that his arguments don't hold water.'

Mr Wilson's party colleague Edwin Poots, meanwhile, has claimed that his views on the formation of the earth have survived last night's deluge intact.

'I fully expect to see a new Giant's Causeway formed by this Great Flood,' he told reporters at a press conference held aboard an ark in his garden.

The North-West has been particularly badly hit by last night's flooding, causing long delays on roads in the Derry and Tyrone areas.

'It'll take hours for our services to get anywhere,' said Translink spokesman Tim Table, 'so no change there then.'

DUP launch 'Club 16–90' budget holidays

In a shock development unrelated to anything in the news, it has emerged that the DUP has plans to launch its own travel agency.

'Club 16–90 will offer attractive holidays whatever your budget, so long as that budget is absolutely humongous and probably provided by someone else,' said the DUP's Travel and Tourism spokesman Thomas Crook. 'We'll have loads of exotic destinations, including the Caribbean, Dubai, Larne and Ballymena.'

There will be some limitations and exclusions to keep the service in line with the party's ideals.

'There'll be no flights on a Sunday,' says Crook. 'All the planes will be chained up at the airport.

'Likewise, in July the only destinations available will be towns hosting the Twelfth.

'And you needn't expect any of those dirty holiday romances either,' he continued. 'It'll be sun, sand, sea and *slacks*, as everyone will have to keep their trousers on at all times.'

Mr Crook has one last word of advice for any potential customers who might want to blow their RHI money.

'When you get to customs, or are meeting with the Parliamentary Standards Authority, and they ask if you have anything to declare, it's important to remember to say "Only my undying devotion to the Queen",' he told us.

'Otherwise it could get messy.'

Adams set to deny ever being Sinn Féin President

Former Sinn Féin chief Gerry Adams has told supporters that he intends to set a date when he'll be able to deny ever having had their support.

'We have a ten-year plan,' he told a party gathering this morning. 'By the time it's finished I'll be able to deny ever existing at all, a bit like unicorns and mermaids.'

The Ulster Fry has gained access to the document and can exclusively reveal Mr Adams's schedule of denial.

November 2017: Gerry announces a date when he intends to stand down as Sinn Féin president, but later that evening denies making the announcement.

December 2017: He posts on Twitter denying that he ever denied the announcement.

January 2018: Gerry reveals that Mary Lou McDonald will replace him as president of the thing he was never president of, after a democratic vote taken at a meeting he didn't attend.

February 2018: Gerry is unable to recognise pictures of Mary Lou McDonald but names Conor Murphy as someone he met once on holiday.

May 2018: During an interview in the Diary Room of *Celebrity Big Brother*, Gerry refuses to admit discussing nominations with *Hollyoaks* star Jorgie Porter.

July 2019: Gerry denies appearing on *Celebrity Big Brother*.

August 2019: Gerry claims that when he said border poll he was referring to the need for a broader pole, as he was concerned that a pillar in his living room wasn't strong enough to support the lintel above.

September 2019: He finally stands down as president of Sinn Féin, and publishes an autobiography detailing his life as leader of the Democratic Unionist Party.

November 2019: Gerry denies knowing who Gerry Adams is during an appearance on a documentary about himself.

January 2020: Gerry Adams is elected president of Sinn Féin.

Better with Sinn Féin
Saoirse Ceart Aontacht

'Paramilitary retirement home' proposed for former Maze Prison site

The news that the Red Hand Commando group has asked to be legalised so that it can become an 'Old Comrades Association' has led to calls for a retirement home specifically for paramilitaries.

'Lots of these guys are getting on in years,' says the brains behind the scheme, Sam Tex. 'Our facility will cater for all Old Age Paramilitaries, regardless of which side they killed for, and they'll feel right at home at the Maze.

'There'll be segregated accommodation, of course – they'd all prefer it that way – but we'll bring them together for traditional retirement home activities.

'For example, we've developed games like Bango – which is a bit like Bingo except the numbers are called in through a coded telephone warning – and Pass the Unattended Parcel.

'We're also planning creative writing classes, so they can learn how to rewrite history, and reminiscence excursions to the towns and villages that they tried to destroy before they retired.'

'Not many people realise this, but we retire like everyone else,' said sixty-eight-year-old Red Hand Commando Wee Willy 'Winkie' Wilkinson. 'I had a lovely leaving do – the lads even presented me with an engraved Glock for the mantelpiece.

Ageing IRA man Slob Murphy agreed with his loyalist counterpart. 'Many of our members are drawing their pensions now,' he told us. 'Quite a few of us got a decent lump sum from that job we shared in the Northern Bank but it's still an armed struggle to make ends meet.'

'All these guys want is to be able to retire and live in peace,' says Tex. 'Although, to be honest, they spent much of their working lives making sure that others didn't have that opportunity.'

Cancelled Ryanair flights to be flown by layabout MLAs

With hundreds of Ryanair flights facing cancellation over staff members' unused vacation time, the Secretary of State has dramatically ordered work-shy MLAs to start earning their wages and take to the skies.

'It's an ideal solution,' he told a press conference earlier. 'Much like pilots, MLAs get paid for sitting on their holes all day. As they've been such doing an excellent job of that recently we thought we'd lean on their expertise to save these flights from cancellation.'

Trials of the scheme have proved troublesome, after the Democratic Union of Pilots, headed by Captain Arlene Foster, refused to fly anywhere that doesn't follow a traditional route. She also ordered cabin crew to march up and down the aisle not selling alcohol.

Meanwhile, Sinn Flyin Deputy First Captain Michelle O'Neill wouldn't allow her co-pilot to take off until she agreed that all cabin announcements would be made in Irish, resulting in a long delay on the runway. Eventually a compromise was reached, but even that left passengers bewildered.

'To be honest, I wasn't really interested in knowing what the windspeed and outside temperature were in the first place,' revealed angry passenger Andy Baggage. 'However I especially couldn't be arsed hearing it in f**cking Irish, English AND Ulster Scots.'

Despite this, Ryanair boss Michael O'Leary has described the experiment as 'a great success'.

'The MLAs have brought all their Stormont skills to our airline,' he told *The Ulster Fry*. 'Just like in your hospitals, the number of passengers on waiting lists has soared, and we're even able to charge kids for the wee bus journey out to the planes.'

Loyalist paramilitaries give themselves forty-eight hours to get out of East Belfast

In a move described as 'highly unusual' by police, loyalist paramilitaries have issued a threat against themselves in East Belfast.

'Apparently it's part of a crackdown on antisocial behaviour,' said Chief Inspector Keith N. Spector. 'They seem to have finally realised that they're the ones doing most of it.'

Prominent loyalist politician Winston 'Winston' Robinson told us that the paramilitaries could no longer sit idly by whilst they were being a danger to their own community.

'We've been at this shite for over forty years now, and we're beginning to sicken our own pish,' he told us.

'I spend most of my time on *Nolan* complaining about problems affecting Protestant working-class areas. Maybe it's time I admitted that my organisation is one of them.'

Since the ceasefires, loyalist paramilitaries have traditionally 'defended their communities' by carrying out attacks on petty criminals and drug dealers, so that they can be petty criminals and drug dealers themselves.

They have also provided valuable support to local businesses, offering to collect a percentage of their takings to assist with the banking process.

Because of these vital public services there are concerns that if the organisations are forced out it will leave a 'power vacuum' in the area, which could filled by shadowy organisations like community groups or even the police.

Local residents, meanwhile, are too afraid to welcome the news.

'Our defenders haven't left yet,' whispered one man.

Two East Belfast men intimidated from their homes by PSNI

Two alleged criminals from East Belfast were forced to leave their homes today after police officers knocked on their doors and intimidated them with the law, *The Ulster Fry* understands.

'They just rocked up and told them they had to leave,' revealed nosey neighbour Michael Keogh-Caine. 'Just point blank told them they had to "get out" cos they'd been arrested.

'Why can't criminal suspects and police officers just get along in this day and age? It's 2018, for gawd's sake.'

The two men were allegedly involved in 'urging' Catholic families to leave their Ravenhill Road homes recently, sparking a tit-for-tat show of intimidation from rival republican ballroots, who then counter-threatened Protestant families to leave theirs.

'It's sectarian f**kwittery the country hasn't seen the likes of since the dark days of last week some time,' confirmed PSNI spokesman Jack Flackett.

The intimidation has been sparked by controversial new research into NI census data, which reveals groundbreaking new evidence that Northern Irish people are either 'Catholic' or 'Protestant', and, most shockingly, that they've been living beside each other for decades – often on the same street.

Cross-community tension group, Sectarian Lives Matter, have since sprung to the mens' defence, however, claiming that all Catholics in the occupied six counties are 'probably in the IRA' and that every Protestant in Ulster is 'most likely a member of the UVF'.

Neither the DUP nor Sinn Féin have condemned the remarks, initially because it would mean doing some actual work – but mostly cos it suits them grand.

NI kids to 'learn about life as an MLA' amid school shutdown

Following last night's eleventh-hour announcement that NI's schoolkids should stay at home this morning, Stormont has reassured parents that their youngsters are getting a unique insight into the life of an MLA.

'We're using this shutdown as an opportunity to find out which NI kids are cut out for a career in Northern Ireland politics,' explained Stormont spokesman Harry Caine. 'Some promising candidates have already emerged actually … although we can't notify them as they haven't got out of bed yet.'

Parents were initially sceptical of the plan, but as the day has gone on, promising indications of political aspirations have been spotted across the country.

'My Dylan has thrown his toys out of the pram three times already today over something daft and ridiculously irrelevant,' revealed excited Newtownards woman Gail Forsythe. 'He maintains he wants to be an astronaut when he grows up, but as soon as this Ophelia shite blows over I'm taking him to a careers advisor to discuss his options.'

This was a view shared by other parents. 'My two are upstairs arguing like f**k over who gets to charge their tablet before the electric goes out,' said Craigavon dad Gusty Fence. 'I've not seen power sharing go like this since the last DUP/Sinn Féin government.'

British government spokesman Grover Turned-Bin confirmed that the kids were gaining all the experience they needed to be MLAs. 'Sitting around on your arse complaining is a big part of the job, as is staying at home when you should be in work,' he told us.

'Any wonder they call it Storm-ont – all they do is produce hot air.'

Stormont launches money-spinning 'adult' chatline

Civil servants have revealed an audacious plan to raise money from the never-ending talks at Stormont by allowing voters to call a special 'dirty' phone line and listen in to the politicians at work.

'These talks have been going on for ages, and no one seems to have a clue what's going on,' we were told by a senior civil servant. 'At the same time there's feck all cash for hospitals and schools, so this kills two birds with one stone.

'Anyone who fancies a bit of hot political action just has to call our 0898 number, then they can listen to all the dirty chat of their favourite politicians.'

The Ulster Fry was lucky enough to get to test the new service, and needless to say we selected DUP leader Arlene Foster first.

'Substantial issues remain to be resolved,' she breathed down the phone. 'Hard … hot … throbbing … substantial issues.'

Unsurprisingly, Gerry Adams answered when we tried to listen to Sinn Féin's Northern Commander Michelle O'Neill.

'I've got a huge mandate,' he moaned. 'No one else's mandate is as big as mine.

'Look at my lovely mandate, don't look at anyone else's mandate, look at *my* mandate, *feel* my mandate,' he continued, before repeating the same phrase in a language similar to Irish.

However Secretary of State James Brokenshire's number was the most revealing, as we overheard him in conversation with Theresa May.

'I know I've been a very naughty boy, Mrs May,' he sobbed over the sound of a swishing cane. 'Please can I come back to London? I promise to never be naughty again.'

Robert Mugabe offered political asylum at Stormont

Plans are being drawn up to secretly fly African dictator Robert Mugabe to Northern Ireland so that he can take up the reins of power in Stormont.

The Ulster Fry understands that, in the absence of a functioning executive, the British and Irish governments have agreed to hand power to the Zimbabwean president, on the grounds that 'he can't do any worse than the last shar.'

The governments hope that Mr Mugabe will be able to raise the Northern Irish economy to the same level as he achieved in Zimbabwe.

'He managed to get inflation to 231 million per cent back in 2008,' says top economist Milton Steriliser, 'which to be fair is a lot less than the increase in the price of Freddos that we've seen here over the last ten years.

'At the same time he raised Zimbabwe's literacy rate to 90 per cent, which is definitely an improvement on the figures we're achieving in East Belfast.'

Mr Mugabe himself is said to be 'looking forward to the challenge', and is drawing up plans to expel all white people from the country.

'That's one way to solve the Irish question,' says Steriliser.

Despite this, local people have welcomed the move with several towns changing their names in honour of the new leader, including Mugabesbridge in County Fermanagh, Mugaberamason outside Strabane and Mugaberry near Lisburn.

'I'm sure he'll do a great job,' said Newtonmugabe woman Victoria Falls.

Gerry Adams to appear on *I'm A Celebrity, You've Got Five Minutes To Get Out Of Here*

After announcing his retirement as Sinn Féin president, Gerry Adams is set to cash in on his new-found free time by taking part in ITV's hit reality show, *I'm a Celebrity, Get Me Out of Here.*

The Louth TD has been installed as an early favourite with the bookies, who predict that the famous Sinn Féin electoral machine virtually guarantees him the win.

'We're already seeing a surge in applications for postal votes,' said one ITV insider. 'Over forty requests came from one address in Fermanagh alone.'

Mr Adams has a variety of tricks lined up to ensure victory.

'Apparently, if he is evicted, he intends to pop back up the next week and just say, "I haven't gone away you know." '

The former West Belfast MP told us that he expected to be named King of the Jungle, but as an Irish republican would refuse to accept the crown.

'Even if I only get 20 per cent of the popular vote I'll still demand that everyone respects my mandate and names me leader,' he told us. 'If they don't, I'll just begin an interminable talks process that drags on till the next series.'

In a related story, it has emerged that Arlene Foster is favourite to replace Adams as Sinn Féin president.

'She's streets ahead of the rest of the field,' says local bookmaker Betty Docket. 'Every time she opens her mouth she adds a couple of hundred votes for the Shinners.'

Next round of Stormont talks to be held in hospital waiting room

Northern Ireland's politicians are to get a dose of reality when the next talks session gets underway, with a proposal to jam them all into a corner in an overcrowded A&E waiting room until they can come to some kind of agreement.

According to reports over Christmas there had been plans to whisk them off to a luxury hotel, in the hope that a round or two of golf and a couple of spa sessions might break the logjam. However these have been shelved amid fears that they might get a bit too comfortable.

'Basically we hope that forcing them to face the grim realities of our overstretched health service might somehow persuade them to get off their arses and actually do what they're paid for,' said our Stormont source. 'It's unlikely, we know, as it would involve them actually thinking about people other than their hard-line "core voters" for a change, but we have to try.'

One problem is that hospitals here are now so full that there may not actually be space for the talks in any of the waiting areas.

'If they're held here, we'll have to erect some kind of tent for them in the car park,' said

Dr Will C. U. Later from the Ulster Hospital. 'It'll have to be squeezed in beside the ones we're putting up for all the extra patients, mind you.'

'That said, an Accident & Emergency Department seems to be the perfect place for these talks,' he continued. 'After all, our politicians are experts in causing both.'

Damning evidence of other extremists sitting in mayor's chair uncovered

As video footage of Britain First's Jayda Fransen sitting in the Belfast Lord Mayor's chair sweeps the internet, city council officers have admitted that several other incidents of known extremists sitting in the same position have been discovered.

'Following this blatant breach we've gone back over CCTV footage and were shocked by what we found,' explained Belfast City Council's Head of Security Albert Clock.

'Turns out that Sammy Wilson sat on it for a whole bloody year in 1986. Then, to make matters worse, when we finally got rid of that wee hur, Doddsy planted his arse during the 90s …

'It hasn't improved much since, to be fair, for we've had "ultra-moderates" like Alex Maskey, Gavin Robinson and Jim Rodgers,' he continued. 'I mean, there was a man who couldn't even jump over a tomato, and he got to be mayor … twice.'

The investigation has since discovered that Belfast City Council has been packed with barely literate extremists for decades, leading officials to issue an urgent warning to Britain First.

'Our message to Ms Fransen is simple,' says Clock. 'We don't need the likes of her coming over here, waving flags, spouting slogans and blaming other people for every problem that affects their community.

'We're perfectly capable of doing that ourselves.'

Stormont on Ice show returns to Belfast

Theatregoers and political pundits are in for a treat today as the long-running *Stormont on Ice* show returns for an astonishing 378th successive performance.

The show sees some of Northern Ireland's greatest play-actors don their ice skates in what has been described by critics as 'an epic talks process in which lots of comedy characters slip about and occasionally fall on their holes.'

'There are some great musical numbers,' says the show's producer Nathan Ever-Happens. 'We have the big hits from *Frozen* of course, like 'Let It Go On, and On, and On', but we've also re-imagined songs from other classic musicals.

'Michelle O'Neill gives a wonderful rendition of 'I Could Have Talked All Night' from *My Fair Lady*, and Sammy Wilson's re-working of Elton John's 'Your Song' from *Moulin Rouge* as 'You're Wrong' is magical.

'Then there are the incredible versions of the *Mary Poppins* classics 'Let's Go Talk Some Shite' and 'Superficial-always-fragile-expandable-talks-process'.

Nathan also explained that there'll be plenty of opportunities for audience participation. 'I'm sure everyone will be on their feet dancing when we all do 'The Time Warp', and there's a fantastic sing-a-long version of 'The Bare Necessities', which is dedicated to the National Health Service.'

'It's the greatest show since *The Sound of Stormont*,' says theatre critic Veloria Kurtins. 'The audiences can't get enough of this cast – they keep bringing them back for repeat performances again, and again, and again.'

'It's like the never-ending story,' says Nathan. 'Which, by coincidence, is the title of the next show from Stormont Productions.'

Adams to spend retirement rewriting history

In an exclusive interview with *The Ulster Fry*, outgoing Sinn Féin president Gerry Adams has revealed that he intends to spend his retirement 'telling the real story of the Troubles'.

'It's important that people know the truth,' he told us. 'If you read the so-called "History Books" you'd think that the IRA did bad things, but they were actually a charitable organisation – that's why I like to call their members "volunteers".

'They spent most of the 1970s engaged in community work, like helping old ladies across the road. Anyone who suggests that they occasionally shot the old lady across the road is a British propagandist.

'Okay, so they engaged in heroic gun battles with heavily armed troops now and again, but they never did anything like batter the living shite out of someone and leave them lying in a ditch.'

Mr Adams told us that it's important that young people learn the truth about the past.

'It's time kids understood that Catholics in the North of Ireland couldn't vote until I negotiated the Good Friday Agreement, by myself.'

Controlling our understanding of the past has become a key battleground in Northern Irish politics, with everyone keen to put a gloss on the role 'their side' played in the conflict.

As well as the work of Mr Adams, DUP leader Arlene Foster is working on a new book called *Why Northern Ireland Used To Be Class Before Themuns Ruined It*, and the British government is planning an official history called *Building Peace: How We Weren't Really Involved in the Troubles But Made Life Better For Everyone*.

Mr Adams' book, *My Role in the Armed Struggle that I Had No Role in*, will be published next year by Fable and Fable.